THE COMPLETE BOOK OF
OUTRAGEOUS AND ATROCIOUS
PRACTICAL JOKES

THE COMPLETE BOOK
OF
OUTRAGEOUS
AND
ATROCIOUS
PRACTICAL
JOKES

BY
JUSTIN GESTE

Illustrated by
Jonathan Bumas

A Dolphin Book
DOUBLEDAY & COMPANY, INC.
GARDEN CITY, NEW YORK
1985

This book is for reading and entertainment purposes only.
The publication of the activities in this book does not
constitute endorsement or encouragement.

A Dolphin Book
Doubleday & Company, Inc.

LIBRARY OF CONGRESS CATALOGING IN PUBLICATION DATA
Geste, Justin.
The complete book of outrageous and atrocious
practical jokes.
"A Dolphin Book."
1. Practical jokes. I. Title.
PN6231.P67G47   1985   818'.5402   85-4451
ISBN 0-385-23044-3

LSI 001

Nolite irasci, aequiperate.
—*Levus Leo*

(Roughly translated) Don't get mad. Get even.
—Leo the Lip

ACKNOWLEDGMENTS

To the following persons whose various contributions helped make this book what it is goes much of the blame. Any lawsuits or grievances you have with these individuals should be directed at them. I sympathize with their parents, schoolteachers past and present, and any other acquaintances. I have no knowledge of their whereabouts either. But for their help, humor and interest, I am very grateful. Keep the cards and letters coming, friends.

Thanks to:

Tim Alexander, Karen Barry, Mary Becilia, Jonathan Birnbach, Norman Birnbach, Derek Blake, Jonathan Bumas, Jack "Sorry Sis' " Carswell, Tim Cripe, Jim Cusick, Joan Ellison, Janis Fitzgerald, Jim Fitzgerald, Casey Fuetsch, Dick Gilroy, Kate Groves, Jaime Harper, Ralph Harper, Scott Harper, Lindy Hess, Gail Kelly, Robert Levy, Chris Lusio, Roy Messersmith, Corinne Montgomerie, Ray Neubauer, Marc Newman, Janet Nolan, Anthony Roussell, Liesl Schillinger, Peter G. Smith, Stacie Strong, Patrick Suchy, Mark Tecotzky, Charles Tinsley, Lisa Wager, Anne Weil, Brian Weiler, Michael Wilkes, Peter Wilson and Robert S. Wilson.

Special thanks to Jeffrey Harper for typing and clerical help.

—Justin Geste

PREFACE

You generally don't find prefaces in books such as this; when you do, they're usually written by third-rate hacks like me who haven't been published in a dog's age and are happy to write whatever fulsome slop and outright lies we're told—just to collect a few dollars of gin money to last us through the week. Be that as it may, I'm still glad to do it.

The Complete Book of Outrageous and Atrocious Practical Jokes is an important literary event, just as is the publication of a novel by Jackie Collins or Judith Krantz. Just as April 15 is a day of rejoicing across the country. Just as Good Friday is a happy day for Christians such as myself.

This book takes the wonder, the magic, the diversity of this planet and largely ignores it. This volume makes *Ulysses* seem like a good book. Refined in sensibility, elegant in style, elegiac in tone—no, this book is none of those things. But, when you've had enough of inconsiderate neighbors, thoughtless roommates, troublesome relatives, rude waiters, scheming colleagues and other brutes who make life unpleasant, this handy volume provides a thorough catalog of ideas to remedy the injustices you've suffered. And all without an expensive lawyer like mine. I only wish this book had been published a year ago. Maybe then I wouldn't be writing this letter from a correctional facility. And my brother-in-law might still be alive. By the way, I'd love to read this book when you're finished.

—Jack "Sorry Sis' " Carswell
San Quentin
September 1985

INTRODUCTION TO THIS FINE BOOK

No need to apologize. We know that you're not the type of person who generally reads books like this; indeed, you rarely read anything except menus and the editorials of *The Wall Street Journal.* Or perhaps you're the type of person who likes big, fat, trashy summer novels—twelve months of the year. Fine. Dandy. You've purchased this book and that's all that matters. We're delighted, mostly because we're not currently collecting royalties on *The Wall Street Journal* or trashy summer novels. (By the way, did you remember to buy extra copies of this book for presents?)

Best of all, you're looking for a good laugh, a deep, rolling "ho-ho-ho" that erupts from your navel and spills up through your chest until, convulsed, you have to sit down on a—whoops!—collapsible chair. But there is more to you than just being a cheap and easy laugh. You are a sexually frustrated, money-driven, brow-beaten, whining, selfish, revenge-seeking citizen —just like us. Congratulations!

You're fed up with those persons for whom removing joy is their expressed and sole function on earth.

You want some protection against the bullies and the oppressors who want to make torture an Olympic event. And so, we'll say it right here: If you are a bully and are reading this, we suggest that you prepare for the worst. Don't think you have any advantage because of your past record of misanthropy. Quit your job, leave school, sell your house, change your name, move to an island the Marines haven't invaded—your days are numbered. We're going to come looking for you.

You may be wondering what kind of persons would collect such an anthology of pranks and stunts. To start, many of us grew up on farms. Boys' Farms. But, in our own defense, let us say that we come from very good families, where the only practical joke committed was convincing the children that they were happy and came from very good families. Huge bills from hundreds of hours in psychiatrists' offices have taught us otherwise. (Whether this experience is a practical joke on our parents is difficult to say.)

A HISTORY OF
THE PRACTICAL JOKE

Practical jokes have a long and detailed history. Little of it is interesting so we shall not discuss it. A crucial time for practical jokes worth noting, however (and other aspects of history we're told), is the French Revolution. Serfs lived horrible lives and worked unconscionable hours—hence, their wake-up call which is still with us: "Serfs up!" Eventually, though, peasants tired of their feudal yoke and rebelled against their masters, slicing off their heads as quickly as one shucks clams (a rather extreme practical joke). The moral of these events is clear: If they can't take a joke, shuck 'em. Ahem.

What is a practical joke and what is not a practical joke? A practical joke is the creation of a comic situation in real life, arising through the use of such techniques as misdirection, prevarication (lying, as it is better known) and the construction of a variety of props and devices. The most famous devices for practical jokes are the joy buzzer and the whoopee or raspberry cushion. The most famous victim of practical jokes is Falstaff. Falstaff is a character in several William Shakespeare plays. (William Shakespeare is the name of a playwright and poet. He is dead.)

To illustrate the difference between what is and what is not a practical joke, we provide the following mild example: Breaking into a friend's dorm room and messing up the papers in his files. This is a small practical joke. Breaking into a hotel room and stealing campaign secrets from files. This is a sizable felony. It is called Watergate. Not understanding this difference caused several people to go to jail and make several million dollars writing about it (a very strange joke on all of us, indeed).

We hope to do the latter without experiencing the

former, so let us say this: We do not advocate your trying any of the outrageous and atrocious acts contained in this book. We do advocate your learning all of them to protect yourself from evil-doers, and we also strongly suggest that you buy many, many, many copies of this book so that your loved ones will also be safe. In doing so, you will make us very happy, and we promise not to play any practical jokes on you. So, if you happen to get in trouble, don't turn around and tell the police we told you to do it. We didn't. We're certainly not going to go to court and give you legal help if that's what you're thinking. After all, we're not H & R Block, for goodness' sakes.

You will note, too, that we have included a reply coupon at the back of the book so that you can write us with your favorite practical jokes, if this volume should prove somewhat less than complete in your opinion. And we emphasize the words "your opinion." So, wherever you are—school, home, the library, plane, train, prison—drop us a line.

THE COMPLETE BOOK OF
OUTRAGEOUS AND ATROCIOUS
PRACTICAL JOKES

LET'S GO TO THE AUDIOTAPE

A New Zealand friend of ours traveled half way round the world to deliver this fitting prank for noisy neighbors. Unable to sleep because of the blaring music, hollering voices and general overwhelming alcoholic din from a party next door, Dennis telephoned his neighbors and politely asked the hosts if they would mind bringing the party inside or keeping the noise level down. Greeted with a slurping howl of derision, he hung up the phone.

Then, taking a suitably receptive microphone and tape recorder, which he placed near the edge of his property, Dennis recorded the irritatingly loud sounds of the party—the yelling, the blasting music and overall mayhem. After a fitful night of sleep, he arose at 6 A.M. and woke his now well-hungover neighbors with the recorded tape of their own party, playing it at full blast on his stereo with the speakers pointed at the neighbors' house.

EXAMSCAM

This devilish practical joke is an excellent antidote for feelings of resentment and frustration that arise when you know that certain persons are stealing exams in advance of a test. So, if you can't bring yourself to report the cheaters to the proper authorities, do what two students at a small college in Maine did.

While the great majority of the class had slogged their way through a difficult economics class that fall, Wendall had barely skimmed the reading and rarely appeared at lectures. He had behaved this way in a number of other classes, but miraculously pulled A's on his exams. Through the grapevine, it was suggested that he was obtaining exams in advance from a number of sources.

James and Daniel went to the library, where they obtained a copy of an old exam from the course. Using liquid paper, they covered the old date and typed in the date for this year's final exam. Then, they photocopied the exam, and with a red pen wrote a variety of notes as if from the professor to his secretary: "Change question 1c to read . . ."; "Have copies of the exam delivered to (department chairman, teaching assistants, etc.)"; "Make 150 copies for exam, on my desk by (exam date), please"; and other notations.

When they were satisfied with their copy, James telephoned Wendall and said, "Listen, I've got a copy of the final exam. Are you interested?"

"You're kidding," said Wendall. "You have it?"

"Yeah, I've got it. Do you want it?"

"Sure, sure."

"Okay, I'll bring it over tonight," said James. "But no one else can be there, or I'll leave."

Acting as if he were a spy handing over secrets, James delivered the "exam" into Wendall's hands that night. "Wendall, no one else gets this but you, right?" whispered James.

"Sure, sure," said Wendall. "What do I owe you, by the way?"

"Nothing," said James. "Knew you needed the help. What's the going rate these days?"

"Oh, five hundred for a real tough one."

"I'd say you're getting a bargain," said James.

Now, they could have left it at that—Wendall with the wrong exam—but instead, sitting around their apartment that night, Daniel asked James, "Do you think Wendall knows what the dean of students' voice sounds like?"

"No, I don't think so. Shall we?"

Daniel picked up the telephone and called Wendall. In a grave voice, he said, "Wendall, this is Dean Howells. The final exam of your economic theory class is missing, and we have reason to believe that you may know something about this matter. I'd like to see you in my office tomorrow morning at eleven."

Wendall flustered and blustered about his total ignorance of anything to do with a final exam. You could *hear* him sweating.

"See you at eleven tomorrow, Wendall," said Daniel in the dean's voice.

Not less than thirty seconds later, James's phone rang. It was Wendall. "You have to do something," he whined. "The dean of students just called and asked about the test. He knows I have something to do with it. Come over here right now."

"I'm afraid you're on your own, Wendall. I'd call my adviser if I were you. That's what they're there for. Advice."

"But you're involved, too!"

"I know. I've already called my adviser. Do you know that your voice is quavering, Wendall?"

"I don't care. Get over here now!"

The next morning at eleven, Wendall, white with horror, arrived at the dean's office.

"Dean Howells, I'm Wendall Harrison."

"Yes," said the dean.

"About your phone call, sir."

"What call?" said the dean.

"Your call last night."

"Oh? I don't remember calling you," said the dean. And then it struck Wendall that the voice didn't sound at all like the one he had heard.

For first-time offenders, you may wish to cut off this stunt at the point at which they are about to call their adviser or visit the dean. For hard-core cheaters, on the other hand, you may just want to let them enter the exam knowing the answers to all the wrong questions.

WHAT'S IN A NAME, or YOU NEVER TOLD ME ABOUT HER

This devilish prank was designed by a schoolteacher named Helen when she learned that her best friend Linda was being two-timed by a man named Frank. At parties where Frank brought his second girlfriend, Helen would respond to the question, "What's the name of Frank's girlfriend?" by saying, "Linda. Go say hello to her. She's awfully shy." The repeated effect of strangers saying, "Hello, you must be Linda" to the other woman will get your message across.

AND NOW FOR MY NEXT TRICK . . .

You are sitting in an expensive restaurant with someone who: (1) Snears at your wine selection; (2) Tells you how much better every restaurant in Europe is, certainly better than your favorite place; (3) Informs you that he/she is leaving you for someone else. When the person excuses himself from the table take a pin and fasten his coat to the table cloth. When you're ready to leave, be sure you stand clear as your dining companion takes his coat and drags the remaining glasses, coffee cups and ashtrays with him.

LOW-CAL NONDAIRY SUBSTITUTE

Shaving cream. An indispensable element in the practical joker's arsenal. It's the perfect whipped topping substitute. Ideal for cream puffs, cakes, sundaes and any other foods that enter the mouths of tasteless cretins. Best of all, it's sugar-free. Contains no saccharin or NutraSweet. Use as directed. Or as you see fit.

STOP IN THE NAME OF THE LAW

Derek, the president of a New York investment company, invited four of his top executives to his fishing lodge on the Canadian side of the Thousand Islands.

The morning after the men arrived for their stag

*When someone sneers at your wine selection
or favorite restaurant . . .*

weekend, a small motorboat pulled up at the lodge's dock and out stepped a constable of the Royal Canadian Mounted Police—a Mountie, as they are better known. He approached the house, knocked on the door and asked to speak to the owner of the lodge. Derek came to the door, while the others in the living room watched.

"Sir," the constable began, "I'm Constable Harris with the RCMP. I'm sorry to bother you, but there's been a fair bit of drug trafficking across the river from the Canadian to U.S. side. Have you seen any small craft crossing at night or any suspicious movement?"

"No," said Derek.

"Any of you?" asked the constable, looking at the men.

They all shook their heads. The constable was now in the living room.

"You're all U.S. citizens?"

"Yes," they said.

"How long will you be here for?"

They told him.

"All right," said the constable, "I'd like to ask you if any of you are in possession of any narcotics."

The men said they were not.

"Okay, could you please bring out your suitcases, and any other pieces of luggage you brought into the house?"

One of the men murmured something about a search warrant.

"We're not in the United States, are we?" said Harris bluntly.

The men went to their rooms and returned with their luggage.

The constable methodically opened each one, carefully turning through the belongings.

"Any camera bags?" he asked.

Two of the men went to their rooms, returned with their camera bags and opened them for inspection. When he had finished looking at them, the Mountie asked, "Is that it?"

"Yes," they said.

"All right, I'm just going to look around a bit." Harris disappeared into several of the rooms. After a minute or two, he returned holding a camera bag. "Whose is this?"

Gerald, one of the guests, looked up and in a quiet voice said it was his. The constable placed the bag on the table before the men and opened it. In one of the compartments he found three plastic bags filled with white powder. Harris looked at Gerald, who froze with terror. He opened the bag, dipped a finger in and dabbed the powder on his tongue.

He looked at Gerald squarely. "You're under arrest," he said.

Gerald leaped from his chair, kicking over the suitcases, and bolted through the door. The constable turned and raced after him.

"Stop or I'll shoot!" called the constable. Gerald

kept running toward the dock. "Stop!" shouted the constable, drawing his revolver. The men watched in horror as Gerald fled toward the dock and three shots rang out. The third shot stopped Gerald in his tracks. The Mountie ran to him.

"Call a doctor!" shouted one of the men.

"You don't need a doctor. He's dead," said the Mountie, walking away from the body. Stunned, shaking, the men watched the constable walk up the stairs of the house. "Everybody sit down," said Harris. The men obeyed. After a minute, the silence was broken. "Something wrong, fellas?" asked Gerald, poking his head through the door. Derek then introduced Constable Harris as an actor he had hired from New York just for this occasion. There was no applause for his performance or for Gerald's.

Outrageous? Yes. Atrocious? Yes. Funny? Not to those men. Not to someone with bad nerves or a weak heart. Some people will do anything to show that they're the boss. Let us recommend that if you are planning to have some friends at a country home for the weekend, forget about this stunt. Stick to the Löwenbräu.

NO MORE FREE LUNCHES

Are you tired of facing the same dreary brown-bagged lunch every day, the same overcooked steam-table staples, overpriced sandwiches and greasy hamburgers, while others in your office take their pals, girlfriends, mistresses, divorce lawyers and each other to expensive restaurants and charge the tab to the company as a business lunch? No? Then you obviously have an expense account. Read no further. You do object? Well, then, you're in business. Send the following memo to the salesmen or executives who abuse their expense account (and break the law, you may haughtily point out). Sign it from their boss.

MEMO TO: SALES FORCE

Eating out with clients is a part of our business as we all know. And, occasionally, so is eating out with friends not directly related to our line of work. Officially, I'm not supposed to recognize this, but it's a fact none of us can afford to ignore right now for a very good reason.

The Internal Revenue Service has targeted our company, in particular our department, for a thorough investigation into expense account

"Ask him *why this isn't a free lunch."*

lunches. They will want thorough diaries and a full accounting of whom you met and what you discussed. May I remind all of you, if you don't already know, that defrauding the Federal Government is a serious crime. The IRS has made it clear that it means business.

I will need from each of you a list of the questionable lunches you have had in the past three months. This is not the time for embarrassment or cover-ups. Lying now can only make things worse for everyone later. I need this list by this afternoon, so that management can develop a coherent strategy to deal with the authorities. There is *no* time for delay. *Do it now.* Failure to do so could jeopardize future employment. For legal reasons, which I'm sure you understand, we are not to discuss this memo among ourselves. Potential questions about past conversations could force someone to perjure himself.

Shred and destroy this memo when you have finished reading it.

If we stick together, we have nothing to fear. Remember, don't let the bastards get you down.

Sincerely,

etc.

No matter what your degree of success with this prank—from momentary terror to full, signed confessions—you are certain to stimulate some personally gratifying excitement in your office.

GOOD CLEAN FUN

We are told that at a recent Shriner convention, a merry prankster poured bubble bath into the hotel fountain. The resulting avalanche of foam proved quite overwhelming, as many beautiful things are in this world.

AREN'T YOU GLAD YOU DIDN'T TASTE IT?

No guide to practical jokes would be complete without this famous stunt. In theory it has all the elements of surprise, deception and outrage that make it a classic. In practice, however—well, read on and see for yourself.

The most common victim for this prank is the crabby neighbor who hates children and threatens to call the police any time kids play within thirty feet of his lawn. The neighbor who screams at children for ringing his bell on Halloween. The neighbor who tells children there's no Santa Claus. We're talking *schmuck*.

A paper bag is filled with fresh dog poop. The bag is set on the victim's front doorstep and set on fire. The doorbell is rung. The creep comes to the front door, sees the burning bag and stomps it out. Meanwhile, the pranksters have run to the back of his house and are pounding on the back door. The creep turns and runs through his house tracking the dog poop across his carpets and floors. Revenge, you say, is sweet.

In theory, yes, but sad to say this is one practical joke we must advise you to never attempt. In this imperfect world where things that can go wrong do go wrong, this practical joke is certain to backfire. The chart below illustrates our point:

ACT	INTENTION	RESULT
Bag of dog poop set on fire.	Man will come stomp it out.	Man not home. House set on fire. You go to jail.
Bag of dog poop set on fire.	Man will come stomp it out.	Man is home. Stomps fire out. Pants catch fire. Burns leg. Sues you and your parents. Go to Boys' Farm.

ACT	INTENTION	RESULT
Knock and holler at back door.	Man will run through house and track dog poop across floor.	Man's feet slippery with dog poop. Takes terrible fall while running through house. Man in hospital. Hires very good lawyer. You and family pay legal fees and damages rest of life.
Set bag of dog poop on fire, run to back door, knock and holler.	Man will come stomp out fire, then run through house and track dog poop across floor.	Man knows this prank. Has played it himself. Waits at back door with shotgun. Blows your head off. You are dead.

BLUE BLOODS

A favorite trick of sorority sisters at Auburn several years ago was to wait for a particularly snooty girl to get in the bath before a big date and then pour bottles of ink into the water. It was not, we hasten to add, indelible ink.

WHERE THERE'S A WILL THERE'S A RELATIVE

This practical joke has a number of applications, but provided the maximum return on investment in the case below. Two brothers, Alan and Peter, lived in a town several hundred miles from their wealthy uncle Horace. Horace was a married man, well into his eighties, with no likely benefactors other than his wife and two nephews.

As Horace got older, his nephew Alan had increasingly attempted to ingratiate himself into his uncle's good graces by writing regularly, visiting at frequent intervals and performing other good deeds. He also bad-mouthed his brother, labeling him irresponsible and lazy and fabricated whopping lies about how he, on the other hand, wanted to extend his uncle's name

*Sorority sisters from Auburn had a favorite
substitute for bath oil.*

TELEPHONE CLASSICS

No book of practical jokes would be complete without the inclusion of those phone calls made by every graduate of practical joker prep school. Below, and throughout the book, we have included a sample of those calls that convinced AT&T that divestiture was the wisest thing to do.

Caller: Hello, is Roy there?
Target: I'm sorry, there is no Roy here.
Caller: Oh, okay. (Hangs up.)

This conversation is repeated five more times during the course of the evening, preferably with different callers' voices.
Finally, you call and say, "Hello, this is Roy. Any messages?"

and wealth into the future through a variety of enterprises he planned to undertake—but only if he had the money to do it. Alan said he had a way, but only if he were in the will.

Aware of his brother's schemes, Peter waited for his uncle and aunt to go away on a holiday and then informed his brother that he had received a cable saying that Uncle Horace had died of a heart attack. Their aunt, he added, could not be reached since she was en route home. Alan immediately sat down and drafted a letter to his aunt, explaining how his uncle intended the will to be rewritten and how Horace had promised him all sorts of money and opportunities. He sent the letter that day. Four days later, Peter told Alan that he had spoken to their aunt.

"How is she?" asked Alan.

"Under the circumstances, I'd say she's okay," said Peter.

Alan called her.

"Hello," answered a male voice.

"Hi, this is Alan, Millie's nephew. Who is this?"

"This is your uncle Horace."

"Who?"

"Your uncle Horace, Alan. We got your letter."

"Oh," said the voice at the other end weakly.

"Sorry to disappoint you, but I'm alive."

There was a long silence at the other end before the phone was hung up.

NAME THAT TUNE

As practical jokes go, this is somewhat tame, but is highly effective at business meetings, awards ceremonies of right-wing organizations and political rallies where taped music is played as an introduction or as part of the festivities. Obtain an official-looking badge, pin or other form of fake credential and inform the sound engineer that there has been a change in the music. Hand him a cassette and give instructions for when the tape is to be played. The Soviet national anthem is a favorite choice because: (1) It is beautiful; (2) It is vaguely familiar (no doubt reminding your targets of the Olympics); (3) By the time the music is recognized little can be done but shrivel with embarrassment; (4) In the best instance, it is the anthem of your target's sworn enemy. At political rallies of Republicans, inserting a tape of John F. Kennedy's speeches or those of FDR could provide a momentary giggle. It is a sad commentary on the Democratic Party to note that inserting a tape of their latest contenders for President could produce embarrassment, too.

FORE! PLAY

This college version of a shivaree comes from the West Coast. While a couple rolled around a dorm room in the throes of passion, a group of young men stood outside the building and tossed a golf ball through the window of the lovers' second-story room. Then, naked except for their golf caps and five irons, the young men climbed through the window. "Do you mind if we play through?" they asked the couple.

TAKING A LAWN SHOT

This joke could only happen among two extremely devoted, pathologically ill practical jokers. After years of playing pranks on George, Stan decided to go for the coup de grâce. He called a landscaping company, introduced himself as George and requested that the landscaper come dig up his front lawn so he could put down new sod and add flower beds and some shrubs. He provided George's address and added that he would be out of town when the work would begin. "My wife, though," he added, "unfortunately my wife is a little unbalanced and she may be difficult or say strange things, but just ignore her if she does. Just start working and ignore her if she makes any trouble."

A week later, the landscaper showed up and immediately went to work on the lawn. After five minutes, George's wife ran to the door and asked, "What on earth are you doing?"

The men, who had been alerted that this woman was unbalanced, just smiled and said, "Oh, nothing. You just go back inside."

"Stop that!" she cried.

"Right," said the men as they dug up some more sod.

"Who told you you could do that?" George's wife continued.

"Your husband."

"He never did!"

"Right." Scoop, shovel, dig. Half the lawn gone.

For fifteen minutes the woman howled, the men smiled and tried to do their work, trying to ignore the oaths, insults and protests hurled at them. Finally, George's wife ran into the house and called her husband.

"There's a gardener here who says you asked him to rip up the lawn."

"What gardener?" said George.

"*Just start working and ignore my wife
if she makes any trouble.*"

FISHING LINE I

Fishing line has proved to be a valuable tool in many practical jokers' kits. Tying all the legs of chairs together at a dinner table is a standard prank that is most effective at formal gatherings. The spectacle of serious business people attempting nonchalance as they pull at their chairs is quite rewarding, especially when they commence a stream of "No, after you, please sit down" that goes right around the table. It should be noted that the humorous effect of this stunt is lost if one of the targets pulls off the back of your mother's prized Louis XIV *chaise* or any other prized family heirloom.

PAVLOV'S PROFESSOR

This highbrow practical joke allegedly occurred at an Ivy League school in a large psychology class and was designed by the graduate students who were teaching assistants. The prank was designed to test the theory of positive reinforcement at a subtle level—to see if persons do in fact pursue behavior that rewards them. The students were told that when the professor (who walked around the auditorium stage when he lectured) stood on the right side, they were to stop looking at him, perhaps whisper or shuffle papers. When he stood on the left side of the stage, they were to be quiet and focus their complete attention on him.

According to our source, by the end of the professor's lecture, he was standing—practically hanging onto—the left side of the stage.

YES, NO, MAYBE

To some this is a party game, to some a controlled practical joke, to others—including ourselves, who have been its target—it is curious, funny, maddening and bewildering. When another game of charades is more than you can bear, suggest this stunt for entertainment.

One person is selected to be the questioner. He is told that he will have to leave the room briefly. When he returns, he will have to discover what secret the rest of the group shares. He can find out the secret by asking questions that can be answered "yes," "no" or "maybe." He must direct each question to a specific member of the group. The questioner is then sent out of the room. When he is out of earshot, you share the secret with the rest of the group. The secret is this: If the person asks a question that ends in a consonant, your answer is "no." If the question ends in a vowel, your answer is "yes." If the question ends with the letter "y," your answer is "maybe." When everyone understands the premise, call the questioner back and let the game begin.

To see how this works, look at the following examples:

Questioner: Mary, do you know the secret?
Mary: No. [The question ended in a consonant.]
Questioner: Mary, you know the secret, don't you?
Mary: Yes. [The question ended in a vowel.]
Questioner: Do you know the secret, Mary?
Mary: Maybe. [The question ended with the letter "y."]

The way this usually works is that the questioner will start by asking a number of reasonable questions—as if he were playing "Twenty Questions" or "Botticelli." He might ask, "Does the secret have to do with an object?" or "Does the secret have anything to do with me?" (Your answers would be, respectively, "no" and "yes.") Eventually, the questioner will start asking you, "Are you enjoying torturing me?" "Yes," you will be forced to respond.

Clues you can give to keep the game moving are: (1) Tell the questioner to ask questions to which he knows the answer, e.g., (to John) "Your name is John, isn't it?" "No," John will say.; (2) If the person is no closer

41

to catching on after that, tell him to ask extremely short questions to which he knows the answer, e.g., holding up an ashtray and asking, "Ashtray?" ("Maybe," you'd reply.)

It is best to pick as questioner a tenacious, inquisitive person with a love of logic, since as the seeming illogic of the answers increases so will the laughter. If you want, you can have two questioners trying to work with each other.

Believe us, this one works. We've been on both sides of it.

YESTERDAY'S NEWS

You're on your own with this one, but our contact Joan insists that there are worthwhile results to be obtained from the prank below. Take a very old newspaper and replace someone's favorite section in the daily paper with it. "The expression is worth a thousand words," she says. She says. We are sorry, but there was not time to test every single prank in this book.

TELEPHONE CLASSICS
THE SOUNDS OF SILENCE

An ingenious prank for a variety of occasions, this stunt was devised by a teenager to repay his parents for grounding him and to avoid the embarrassment of hearing his parents tell his friends on the telephone, "I'm sorry, John can't come to the phone or go out. He's grounded."

John reacted by going to each phone in the house, removing its cover and detaching the wire that activates the bell. Then he put the phone back together. Thus, if you picked up a phone to make a call, it worked. But no incoming calls would be answered, since no one would hear the bell.

No doubt some of you want to know how to identify this wire. All fine and dandy, but since this book is strictly for entertainment only and since we don't want you to be electrocuted, we're going to keep mum on this one and leave it to qualified experts to figure it out.

DON'T SAY WHAT THIS REMINDS YOU OF

At a liberal arts college in Maryland, students rented a crane and scrounged dumps for several dozen old tires. In the middle of the night, they engaged in an industrial version of ring toss, using the main flag pole on campus. In the morning, the administration discovered a forty-foot tower of vulcanized rubber. For a few minutes heads were scratched and the question was asked, "How do you get them off?"

IMPROPER BUSINESS CONVENTIONS

Many hotel guests, exhausted by a day's travel or business on the road, have arrived in their rooms ready to sleep, only to find that a boisterous group of conventioneers is occupying an adjoining suite. From the decibel level penetrating the wall it appears that it is a convention of howling banshees and heavy metal rock groups. When calls to the front desk and polite requests yield no reduction in the shrieking and music, one must often do without a good night's sleep.

One source has reacted to this inconsiderate behav-

In the morning the administration discovered
a forty-foot tower of vulcanized rubber.

ior by rising early in the morning, finding out the name of the convention group, then methodically going through the hotel to the group's meeting rooms and attaching a printed notice to the doors that reads "Meeting moved to Suite 1122" or some other nonexistent place. Any notices installed by the hotel are removed or altered to add to the confusion.

Another irate hotel guest with artistic flair distributed photocopies of a notice around a convention room before his targets arrived. The notice read: "Just Opened! Jezebel's Bar and Restaurant! Jezebel's welcomes (name of the group) and invites all of you to a special night on the town. All you can drink for $5 from 9:30 to 11:00 P.M. tonight. Live music and dancing. Located at (address on outskirts of town). Come one, come all!"

Naturally, there is no such place as Jezebel's.

Our friend notes that if a nursing school exists in the city where one is staying, one should provide the fake address as being next to the school and mention this fact in the notice, since nurses and cheap booze-ups figure prominently in the fantasies of many conventioneers.

CONFOUNDING CONFETTI

"Small is beautiful" is the operating maxim for this delightful little prank, especially designed for office use. The one requirement is that there must be an overhanging light fixture in reasonable proximity to the target's chair. An overhanging beam or any other object on which you can place a small (3″ × 3″) box will do as well.

First, attach a good-sized elastic band to the bottom of the small cardboard box. Second, fill the box with confetti or rice. Third, enter the target's office while he is absent. Next, take the elastic band and twist it several times so that it is wound up, without bunching up on itself. Then take the free end of the elastic band (the other is attached to the outside bottom of the box) and attach the free end to the underside of the overhanging light fixture. Now attach a very fine thread to the box. This is your trigger, which you will take with you, so bring enough thread to reach from the target's office to wherever you're going to execute the prank. Finally, place the small box loaded with confetti on *top* of the light fixture or overhanging beam. The elastic should be long enough to do this without stretching it.

If you've correctly followed these simple steps, this

is what you have: a small box filled with confetti on top of a light fixture. The bottom of the box is connected to a wound elastic that runs to the underside of the light. Attached to the side of the box is a long thread. You take the end of this thread and leave the office.

When your target returns to his desk and sits down, you pull the thread from wherever you are. The box falls off the light fixture; the elastic unwinds, spinning the box and confetti everywhere; and your target has no idea where the stuff is coming from.

One of the advantages of this prank is that it is impossible to trace it to its source—unless, of course, you're foolish enough to use easily visible thread and pull the stunt from your desk.

STILL WATERS RUN DEEP IN SLEEP

This camp activity is as popular as whittling and is about as sophisticated. A sleeping target's hand is immersed in a pan of warm water. In a moment, through the self-liquidating miracle of nature herself, so are the target's shorts. The British have a coarse expression for embarrassing someone or bringing a person down a notch or two. It is known as "letting the piss out of him." It is not known whether this prank is the source of the phrase.

SOMETHING BUGGING YOU?

Do you have friends who do not recognize the difference between clutter and dirt? Refer to you as a slob because you do not have a desk organizer in each drawer? Shriek if they find one dirty glass in your sink? This small, simple prank silences your critics.

Next time you are invited to a dinner at the home of the excessively fastidious, prepare by placing two live insects—large cockroaches are excellent, as are beetles or waterbugs—into a pill vial. As your host prepares to sit down for the main course, wait for him or her to be distracted before releasing the insect friends on the table. This can be surreptitiously done by placing the pill vial under your napkin and releasing the bugs as you pick up the napkin and empty vial in one motion.

After the first mention of the insects, you might add, "Oh, how nice. More hors d'oeuvres."

"Oh, how nice. More hors d'oeuvres."

REACH OUT AND TORTURE
SOMEONE I

Sam had asked his neighbors on several occasions if they would mind not playing King Crimson records at full blast between the hours of one and five in the morning, since he had a well-established habit of sleeping at night. No amount of polite requests or knocking on the paper-thin walls produced any response. So, for several days at a time, Sam would move to a friend's apartment. En route, he would stop by an out-of-the-way pay telephone and call his apartment, where his phone lay by the wall set to ring at its loudest. He would then leave the phone off the hook and walk away. During the day he would periodically check in to see that his line was still busy as the phone rang and rang and rang. Sam's neighbors now play chamber music and drink herbal tea between five and seven o'clock in the evening.

Sam has additional suggestions for persons mauled by their neighbors' noise. Hook up a microphone to your speakers and place the microphone by the phone. Face the speakers toward your neighbors. Return after a couple of days of steady ringing and ask your neighbors if you'd missed any calls.

STOOL PIGEON

An editor for a publishing company has set the tone for his department by using this prank as an introduction to new employees. Our editor Jim approached a young man the first day he arrived at the company and said, "Hello, I'm Ted Johnston from personnel. Glad to have you here. Sorry to have missed you earlier at your first personnel meeting. Welcome to (name of company). I don't know if anyone's told you, but you will be getting a company physical—a full once-over—and we'll need some stool samples as a preliminary today to rush over to the lab so that they can schedule your appointment. So I'll leave these paper cups with you and this paper bag. When you're finished, take the samples down to the personnel office and put them on Mrs. Peacock's [the personnel manager] desk when you're ready."

Jim swears this has worked.

PARTY LINE

Of all telephone pranks conceived, this perhaps is the most ingenuous, crafty, perplexing, bizarre and often hilarious. To execute this practical joke, a telephone

TELEPHONE CLASSICS
WHERE THERE'S A
WALL . . .

A call to anyone not named Wall.

Caller: Hello, is George Wall there?
Target: No, there is no George Wall here.
Caller: Mary Wall?
Target: No, there's—
Caller: Andy Wall?
Target: Look, I—
Caller: Stan Wall?
Target: No—
Caller: You mean there are no walls at your house?
Target: Yes.
Caller: Well, if there are no walls, what's holding up the house?

with two extensions is required. The most easily adapted for this prank is that model with buttons that are depressed to get a different line. (There is often a "Hold" button on these models as well.) By taking the telephone apart, the two lines can be connected so that two different outgoing calls can be placed at the same time. (Again, the details of how exactly to do this are going to be kept a secret. Our intention is to amuse, not dismantle the nation's communications system. We are not, after all, the Luddites.)

Once the two lines are connected, you are ready to go. If you are working alone, you need only dial the first six numbers of one target's phone number, place it on hold, quickly dial the other target's number on the other line, then switch back and dial the seventh number of the first target's phone number. Then press down the buttons for both lines and listen to both phones ring. (Mechanical ingenuity can show you how this is possible.)

If you are working with an accomplice, you can each dial on separate extensions a different person at the same time, provided one of you has connected the two lines on his phone. Thus, you both dial your different numbers on different phones at the same time, and, *voilà*, both phones at the other end begin to ring at the same time. Both persons who receive the call think the other has phoned him or her. So, if one of you calls your mother and the other calls your father, both your parents will pick up a ringing phone and ask why the other called. If a person has an answering machine at home, you can call him at work, while your accomplice calls your target's answering machine. The result is the bizarre experience of your target receiving a call from his own answering machine. You can connect old lovers, new lovers, students who cut class with their teachers, criminals with the police and any unlikely couple you deem fit. Remember, though, the persons you call can hear your voice on the line. You are essentially creating a conference call with your fiddling. See how practical this book is? To show how far this prank can be taken we offer the following true-life example, committed by two pranksters against an antagonist of theirs, here called Wanda.

Wanda had just submitted her undergraduate thesis on barbecue (yes, a thesis on barbecue) to her professor, so John and Alan began by connecting Wanda to her teacher.

"Hello," said the professor.

"Hello," said Wanda.

"Who are you calling?" asked the professor after a pause.

"Who are *you* calling?" asked Wanda.

"Lady, you called me," said the professor.

"No, I didn't. You called me," said Wanda.

"I certainly didn't. My phone just rang."

"So did mine."

"There must be some problem. Where are you calling from?"

"Hunter County," said Wanda.

"That's where I am," said the professor.

"I'm in Hattersville," said Wanda.

"So am I."

"I'm calling from Monroe College," said Wanda.

"I'm at the faculty building in my office."

There was a pause.

"Professor Burns!" said Wanda.

"Who's this?" asked Professor Burns.

"Wanda Adams."

"Why did you call me?"

"I didn't. My phone rang. I thought you called me," said Wanda.

"I didn't."

Another pause.

"You have my thesis, don't you?" asked Wanda.

"Yes, but I haven't read it. I only got it yesterday."

"Right. I didn't expect you would have. All right, good-bye."

"Good-bye," said the professor.

John and Alan called Wanda back, connecting her this time with a pizza parlor.

"Hello," said Wanda.

"Hello," said an employee at the pizza parlor.

"Yes?"

"Do you want to order?" asked the voice.

"Order what?" asked Wanda. "Who do you want to speak to?"

"Nobody. You called here. We're a pizza parlor."

"You called *me*," said Wanda.

"No, I didn't. You called me. The phone rang."

"So did mine," said Wanda.

"Lady, we're a pizza parlor. We don't call people to see if they want to make an order."

"Forget it. Good-bye." Wanda hung up.

This time John and Alan connected Wanda to the college switchboard.

"Who is this?" asked Wanda in perplexed tones.

"Monroe College switchboard. Can I help you?" said a woman.

"Why did you call me?" asked Wanda.

"Madam, you called me. Can I help you."

"But my phone just rang. Why did you call?"

"Madam, the college switchboard does not make outgoing calls."

After connecting Wanda to Alcoholics Anonymous, John and Alan called her directly.

"This is the telephone company calling," said Alan. "We understand that you're having some problems with your line."

"Thank God. Yes," said Wanda, relieved.

"We're also told that you're playing some sort of prank on persons in your calling area. Would you please stop this immediately?"

"I'm not playing any prank. I keep getting calls from people who say they're not calling me."

"All right, whatever. We're going to do some work on the line in your area. For a few minutes the wires

57

will be exposed to the lineman on the job. So, if your phone rings, please don't pick it up, since that could cause the lineman to be electrocuted."

"All right," said Wanda reluctantly.

Then, as you no doubt have guessed, John and Alan called her back. (See "Reach Out and Torture Someone II or The Wichita Lineman Is Dead on the Line.") After failing to respond on several occasions, Wanda finally gave in and picked up the phone.

"Aaaaiieeeeeee!" screeched Alan, in a highly realistic impersonation of a lineman being electrocuted. Wanda screamed and dropped the phone.

After a few minutes, they called Wanda back.

"This is the telephone company," said Alan. "Did you answer the phone?"

"Yes," said Wanda weakly, "I thought—"

"The lineman we told you about has been severely electrocuted."

"Oh, no."

"Oh, yes. We and lawyers will be in touch with you soon, you can be sure." Alan hung up.

Next they connected Wanda with the real phone company.

"Hello," said Wanda, tiring rapidly.

"Hello," said a man at the phone company.

"Who is this?" asked Wanda.

"It's the phone company."

"I'm so glad you called back. What's going on?"

"Ma'am, we didn't call you. You called us."

"No, I didn't. My phone just rang. Aren't you calling about my broken phone?"

"I'm sorry, ma'am, but we have no way of knowing a phone is broken unless a customer calls us."

"But you just called me about the fellow being electrocuted."

"I'm afraid we didn't," said the man, convinced he had some loony on the phone—which was not far from the truth.

When that conversation ended, John and Alan connected Wanda back to the pizza parlor, a crisis hotline and finally back to her professor Burns.

"Hello," said the professor.

"Hello," said Wanda.

"Adams, what is it now?"

"Professor Burns—"

"Wanda, I have not had time to grade your thesis, so you needn't call me."

"But I didn't call you. My phone rang. Something crazy is going on."

"Get some sleep, Adams."

"Professor, I didn't call you."

"Okay. Good-bye."

Finally, Wanda was connected back to the phone company. In the midst of that conversation, though, Alan let go a burst of laughter which in an instant identified him to his target.

"Alan!" Wanda screamed.

The pranksters fled to their rooms. (They were working out of the student newspaper office.) Five minutes later, John received a call. It was Alan.

"John," came the plaintive whisper.

"Alan?"

"Yes."

"Why are you whispering?"

"I'm in my closet."

"Why?"

"Because Wanda is outside my room pounding on the door and won't stop."

"Oh," said John. "Well, you can do one of two things. One, tell her it's part of a psychology experiment on stress. Two, tell her the truth."

Alan ended up lying. Wanda never spoke to him for the rest of the semester. John told the truth and was forgiven—or partly forgiven.

ENGINE BLOCK

Another excellent technique for preventing someone from driving while intoxicated or from pursuing you should you be making a getaway is to jack up the back of the target's car and place wooden blocks under the back of the car, so that the rear wheels are about four inches off the ground. When the individual gets in his car and puts it in gear, he will wonder what malfunction is keeping him from moving, as his wheels spin in the air.

Naturally, if the person has front-wheel drive, you will have to place the blocks under the front end of the car for the prank to work. If you are especially determined to keep this person from driving, obtain the target's keys and remove his jack from the car.

IF YOU'VE GOT AN ITCH, SCRATCH

A staple of summer campers across the country is this prank in which toothpaste is squirted into the hand of a sleeping target. His head is then scratched, sending his undiscriminating brain to work. His toothpaste-laden hand goes to his head and smears toothpaste across his face. And you thought the Three Stooges could be stupid.

I BEG YOUR PARDON

This act of outrage occurred several years ago at the University of Wisconsin at Madison. A former U.S. President had recently resigned from office under a dark cloud of scandal and suspicion. Although not

Should you be making a getaway,
an excellent technique . . .

formally charged with any crime, Dick was immediately pardoned by his successor for any crimes he may have committed. This generous successor had been, of course, appointed by Dick.

That spring, at the University of Wisconsin at Madison, in response to a right-of-center campus newspaper challenge, a group of students constructed a banner and, using papier-mâché and black yarn, a five-foot phallus.

Using special tools, in the early hours of an April 1 morning a climbing expert scaled the outer wall of the tallest building on campus, the administration building—fourteen stories high.* Upon reaching the tenth floor, he hoisted the phallus and the banner, securely attaching them to the building. The climber then descended undetected.

It was not until late morning that university officials removed the banner and sculpture. By this time the entire campus had been exposed to the oversized phallus and banner, which read, "Pardon my dick, too."

* Note: It is stunts like this that force us to reiterate that this compendium of pranks is for reading pleasure only and not to be considered for execution.

THE SOAP THAT FLOATS IN WATER

Replacing the contents of soap dispensers with vegetable oil is a lowly but popular campus prank. Other variations include replacing powdered soap with powdered paint or liquid soap with motor oil. Use these only if you're really desperate.

CLOSET BULLIES

As we said in the introduction, this book can provide relief from bullies and other tormentors when no civilized form of redress exists. This next prank proved to be an effective substitute for costly lawyer fees and a handy way of dealing with a bully.

Several members of an Oklahoma City office grew tired of Floyd's unprovoked practical jokes and general harassment. It was also known that Maryanne, one of the secretaries, was scared of going down to the supply closets in the basement. Ken, one of her co-workers, approached Floyd.

"Hey, Floyd," he said, "I've got a great idea. Maryanne has to go down to one of the supply closets in a few minutes, and you know how scared she is of that place. This is what we'll do. I've got the keys to the closets, and we'll all hide in different ones. When she comes down, we'll all jump out and scare her."

"Wild," said Floyd. "I love it. Let's do it."

Ken, Floyd and another colleague went down to the basement. Ken took out the keys and opened the supply closet Maryanne would be visiting. "Okay, Floyd, you hide here and scare Maryanne, and we'll get in the ones down the hall and get her on the way back."

"I love it," said Floyd. "Let's do it."

"Hurry up, she's coming," said Ken.

Floyd got in the closet and closed the door. Ken locked it (the door could not be opened from the inside). The other two then went back to their desks. Maryanne, by the way, had no intention of going to the supply closet that day. Floyd was released later in the afternoon.

An excellent variation on this stunt is to lock up your target and then create an excuse that gets his boss to go down to the supply closet. While you may unfairly scare the boss, imagine your target's surprise when he finds out who's at the door.

NO CAUSE FOR ALARM, STUDENTS

This popular parochial school prank requires several alarm clocks all set to go off at different times during a class. Hide the clocks in the wastebasket under piles of paper, in empty desks, the teacher's desk or the supply closet. Watch the teacher try to find the hidden clocks. This prank has prompted some teachers to opt for early retirement. Other teachers simply resort to a parochial school's historically favorite source of inspiration: the yardstick.

TRIAL BALLOONS

This practical joke is as well-known and well-loved as any Longine Symphonette or Slim Whitman album. Fill an entire room, office or car with balloons. Blow the balloons up first, though. Otherwise the prank is not quite as funny as it might be. It falls sort of flat. Just blow up the balloons first.

A favorite stunt of blowhards.

A DAY YOU'LL ALWAYS REMEMBER

This atrocious act was committed at a wedding by a lover spurned for a wealthy suitor. It is not known whether the practitioner is still alive. We sort of doubt it.

At a very prestigious wedding in Cleveland, a large congregation observed a high Episcopalian ceremony involving the children of two prominent families—Skip and Muffy Somebody (we weren't told).

In the midst of the vows, the time came when the priest asked if there was anyone who saw any reason why these two people should not be joined in holy matrimony let him speak now or forever hold his peace—and a man in the back of the church rose and said loudly, "I do!"

"I have had frequent sexual relations with the bride in the last two weeks, as have several of my friends. Only last week the groom spent the night with my sister whom he has impregnated once before," intoned the man as he walked up the aisle. "This wedding is a sham, the groom is a womanizer, the bride is a—" His voice faltered and he froze halfway up the aisle.

"Sorry, wrong wedding," he gasped and then fled the church.

SOUP IS GOOD FOOD, or
TOP THIS, LINDA BLAIR

When you find it necessary to disrupt a pompous gathering, shock the snobs or clear a room, this outrageous act is a sure-fire winner. It is not for the faint at heart. Open a can of vegetable beef soup and pour it into a plastic bag. Seal the bag and conceal it on your person. When you arrive at the function you have targeted, wait for a sizable crowd to gather. Then, off to the side, commence a stream of wretching sounds as you pour the vegetable soup on the floor or table. (Dedicated practical jokers often disappear into the bathroom before pulling this stunt and fill their mouths with some of the soup to provide a heightened sense of reality and drama.)

As all eyes turn on you, leaning over the mess wretching, you may pause as if waiting for assistance. At the point when someone asks the inevitable question, "Are you all right?" or asks if he can help you up, say, "Just one minute, please." Take a plastic spoon out of your pocket and shovel some of the soup into your mouth. Then get up, smile and add, "I'm much better, thanks."

DEATHLY ILL

Since you're reading this book purely for amusement, we needn't tell you that this next stunt is not at all funny if played on someone who is in poor health. A woman named Joan has perpetrated her share of pranks and enjoys this one especially. Several times during the course of a day, she tells a friend that he or she doesn't look very well. Then she places red food coloring in the toilet tank. "When the person flushes," our source notes, "he will be convinced that he hasn't long to live."

Joan, if only you had used your powers for the forces of good instead of evil.

NOTHING PERSONAL, BUT . . .

This highly amusing prank was committed by a group of speechwriters in a large bank north of the border and can be practiced in any city whose newspaper publishes a Personals or Companions column. It is an essentially victimless prank, but this fact should not dissuade you from having fun with it. Circulate the following memo in your office, adapting it as necessary.

MEMO
SUBJECT: Personals Column—The Star

Jill Robbins is having a birthday on Wednesday, September 29. She will be twenty-nine, it is rumored (Jill started the rumor), and we her colleagues want to help make it an exciting occasion.

It occurred to some of her friends that Jill might like to meet a lot of lovely new chums, or at least get a birthday letter from them. We propose to submit the following ad to the Personals column of the *Star:*

AD

> Help! My twenty-ninth birthday is just around the corner—barely a year before the big "Three-O." Petite, fun-loving blonde seeks to make loads of new friends. I'm ready for adventure! Tell me why we'd enjoy an evening together and please include picture and phone number. (If group pictures, send only one phone number.) Can't wait to hear from you—please write today.

You can help by:
1) Not mentioning this to Ms. Robbins.
2) Writing a letter yourself to the *Star* in response to the ad. Please include an explanation for pictures in which black tape covers the eyes. Also

please check with me if you wish to write as the president, vice-president or treasurer of our company. The last time something like this was done, the recipient received eighteen letters from the president, all in different handwriting. This kind of thing will make Ms. Robbins suspicious. Only one fake president, please, and if the real president of our company wishes to write, he should not use his real name.

We plan to present the resulting bushel of mail to Jill at a local watering hole after work on her birthday. Please join us. Feel free to pay for your own drinks.

The resulting party should be an amusing one, unless one of your colleagues shows your boss the letter you wrote using his or her name. Or uses your name and shows the letter to your wife.

TELEPHONE CLASSICS FROM THE DAYS OF YESTERYEAR

Older readers will remember that at one time Prince Albert was the brand name of a well-known tobacco and the subject of this Golden Oldie.

    Caller: Do you have Prince Albert in the can?
    Store Owner: Yes.
    Caller: Well, then, let him out!

COULD IT BE . . . MY BREATH?

After dinner at his home, Dennis suggested to his friend Harry that they play a game of pool downstairs. "I don't play much," apologized Harry, "but I'll give it a go." After losing the first match, he suggested playing for money, "just to make it interesting."

"Fine, if you'd like," said Dennis.

"Fifty dollars too much?" asked Harry.

"Okay," said Dennis.

The above is not a practical joke. It is called a hustle. Harry promptly won fifty dollars from his host. Dennis politely excused himself from the room. When he returned he asked Harry if he could borrow his keys to move his car out of the driveway. When Dennis returned several minutes later, they played another game of pool before Harry excused himself to meet a girlfriend.

It was to be a romantic first date, yet en route to a favorite parking spot with his lady friend, Harry detected a faint unpleasant odor. When he arrived at his romantic rest area, prepared to make his advances, the smell became unbearable. His plans were foiled and he returned home, embarrassed. When he got out of his car, his nose led him to the trunk. He opened it and found Dennis's rotting five-day-old garbage.

SAY WHAT?

This inspired prank is particularly effective with the excessively polite. When setting up a meeting or rendezvous with two mutual acquaintances who do not know each other, tell one of them privately, "The man (or woman) you are meeting is hard of hearing, and is very embarrassed by it. So be sure to speak loudly so he can hear you. And try to act naturally, since he's very sensitive about his hearing loss. Please, whatever you do, don't mention his hearing."

Then call the other person and tell him the same thing. The sight of two persons sitting in bar, restaurant or other public place speaking loudly and with great enunciation while trying to act relaxed is highly comical.

(It must be said, however, that groups of actors who are not hard of hearing are known to do this frequently in restaurants. The effect in this instance is not comical, but simply annoying.)

ESPECIALLY FOR YOUR PROTECTION

It is difficult to believe that in an era of sisterhood and of the word women being spelled "wimmin" (a very bad joke indeed) that the following stunt was committed by a woman against members of her sex. But this happens to be the case. In fact, the prank was committed at Smith College, the oldest women's secretarial college in the country. Maybe the prankster was jealous. Maybe she's a lesbian (a very good practical joke on men).

Particularly effective with the excessively polite.

She obtained sheet stationery from the college health service and wrote the following letter:

Dear Students:

It has come to our attention that a manufacturing defect exists in all diaphragms issued by the college health services between the dates of September 28 and February 14 of this college year. To prevent any unforeseen occurrences, do not use these diaphragms. They are not safe or effective. If you were issued one of these contraceptive devices between these dates, please place the diaphragm in an envelope and deposit it in the red box outside the Student Union on Tuesday, March 10, between the hours of 10 A.M. and 2 P.M. This is necessary for the college to deal effectively with the manufacturer. We regret any inconvenience.

Sincerely,
College Health Services.

The rascal delivered photocopies of the letter to all the dorms, placed the red box by the student union and watched. A rumor, which has been confirmed as absolutely false, is that this prankster's name is Phyllis Schlafly.

SIGNS OF TROUBLE

One New England woman suggests placing "For Sale" or "Rooms for Rent" signs on neighbors' lawns. It is not nice to include their phone number on the sign, especially if the neighbors are away.

A variation on this may be to place "For Sale" or "Wanted" ads in newspapers. Be sure to make them apropos: The new cat your girlfriend recently purchased would go in as a "Cat for Sale" or the apartment someone recently found would yield a "For Rent (at a far-below-marketplace value to encourage more callers) Immediately."

PRACTICAL JOKE PENTATHLON

A group of Boston pranksters included five different pranks in this one stunt practiced against one of the perpetrators' roommates during her freshman year. As Cyndi Lauper would say, "Girls just want to have fun."

The ingredients for this prank were: a large piece of plastic; copious amounts of Jell-O; Marshmallow Fluff; a hideously ugly, hairy mask; Scotch tape; and about ten pennies.

While Lynn peacefully slept, her roommate Donna quietly left the room. Waiting outside were her fellow "floor mates" with the tools and accessories. First, one person quietly entered the room and turned the main electrical switch in the closet off—effectively cutting off all power in the room. The cord connecting the handset to the rest of the phone was removed, and the dial tone button was taped down. Marshmallow Fluff was smeared on the mouth- and earpiece. Out in the hallway, a pile of Jell-O was dumped on the plastic and dragged quietly into the room and placed by the target's bed. Next, one of the collaborators donned the ugly mask and slipped into the bed Donna had vacated, while the others stood outside the door and "pennied" the two inside the room. (As old as short-sheeting a bed, "pennying a room" involves squeezing pennies between a door and its frame. By creating enough pressure, the door cannot be opened from the inside.)

The prank was then set in motion. From next door, one of the team called Lynn's room, while the others listened outside. The phone rang. Lynn got up to answer it—stepping into the warm, slimy, slippery Jell-O . . . screamed . . . went to answer the phone . . . picked up the phone, smearing her face with Marshmallow Fluff . . . the phone continued to ring, since the dial tone button was taped down . . . Cursing, Lynn went to the wall and turned on the light switch

. . . the room remained dark . . . she called her roommate to get some help . . . no response . . . leaning over her roommate's bed she hollered . . . but, alas, rising from the bed was the hideous masked face, reflected in the dorm-room window . . . With a shriek Lynn bolted to the door, which wouldn't open . . . more shrieking and hollering . . . until the masked monster removed her disguise and asked, "Was it something I said?"

IT WOULD BE CHEAPER TO SEND THANK-YOU NOTES

A man named Alan grew tired of hearing his friends Tony and Jane, who lived together, discuss wedding plans which never came to pass. With several like-minded associates, they waited for the couple to take a week's trip abroad before distributing an invitation which read:

Mr. and Mrs. Dennis Smith
Request the pleasure of your company
At the marriage of their daughter
Jane Marie
on the 25th of October, 1984
at two o'clock in the afternoon

St. Paul's Church
North Meadowbrook

When the couple returned, they found dozens of wedding gifts awaiting them and wondered whether the wages of sin were worth resisting this bribe. They sent the gifts back.

THE FOOD THAT FILLS YOU UP AS IT EMPTIES YOU OUT

For the obvious health dangers involved, we take a dim view of this prank, but since we have received correspondence from sorority sisters at Auburn, students at University of Tennessee and others telling us that this was a standard stunt, we feel the heavy obligation to include it to make the collection as complete as possible.

To show the fraternity brothers who snubbed you that there are no hard feelings, send them a box of brownies, made with a chocolate flavored laxative. Their gratitude will be short-lived, to say the least. Ha-ha. Next, please.

THE GREEN, GREEN GRASS OF HOME

A practical joker from Virginia with a green thumb and keen sense of mischief advises that for this prank to work the target must be out of town for at least two weeks while the practitioners carry out their fun.

Once the target has left town, you and your associates gain access to his room, accompanied by one or two wheelbarrows full of topsoil, a bag of grass seed and some plastic sheets. Spread the plastic sheets across the floor and cover them with about an inch of the topsoil. Next sprinkle the grass seed evenly across your newly created garden, avoiding areas (e.g., under the bed) where the grass will not grow. Finally, water the freshly sewn seed, making sure not to get it too wet.

Don't forget to leave the window shades up. You want to ensure the best possible lighting. If you think it's necessary, go ahead and put some grow lights in the room. There's no sense in taking chances with new seed. You may also want to support your efforts by including one of those Miracle-Gro fertilizers in the soil.

Upkeep of the garden simply requires that you come back every couple of days to make sure the grass has

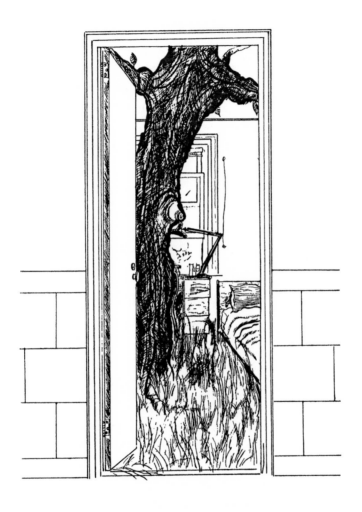

For practical jokers with a green thumb . . .

enough water. With any luck, your target should return to a carpet of lush green grass about three or four inches high. Do not, as a wry joke, leave your target a set of grass trimmers. He may very well stab you with them.

BOWL THEM OVER

This vulgar prank is a classic nonetheless. Stretch a sheet of clear plastic wrap across the toilet bowl. After the folks have gone to bed. At a target's beer party. Best not to get too close to the scene of the crime.

PEARL HARBOR COMES TO MINNESOTA

Michael attended a small college in Minnesota that we'll call St. Offal's. On top of his dormitory sat air raid sirens that had been installed during World War II. Had they ever been used for broadcasting they would have made radio obsolete in Minnesota.

Deciding that these speakers needed a new purpose in life, Michael enlisted the help of his roommate, whose dexterous cellist's fingers and a slender metal file provided access to the attic that housed the siren's machinery. Accompanied by a sound engineer, they attached the air raid sirens to a transmitter and ran wires through a small hole in the wall and down a drainage pipe. The pipe conveniently dropped three stories down outside Michael's dormitory room, where it slithered in through the window and attached to his stereo.

On a Tuesday at 3 A.M. the seven hundred residents of his dormitory were treated to the opening measures of the theme from *2001: A Space Odyssey.*

Two weeks later, on a Thursday at 6 A.M., the residents were awakened to a fully orchestrated version of "The Star Spangled Banner." The system proved fully functional and was ready for its main performance.

The Saturday after the national anthem episode, St. Offal's held a picnic for students, alumni, faculty and friends on the lawn in front of Michael's dormitory. The picnickers ate, drank and threw Frisbees in the Minnesota springtime sun. Suddenly, from above came an increasingly loud drone of engines—of airplanes. Then the sky erupted in the rattle of fighter planes on strafing runs, ripping off rounds of ammunition that screamed and sputtered into the earth. Caught in the middle of the field, some picnickers began to race for cover, others sprawled on the earth, facedown—except the dean of the college, who ran toward Michael's dormitory. The sounds of the airplanes abruptly stopped.

Michael's system provided various forms of auditory entertainment that year and the next. When Michael left the residence, so did the Christmas carols, the

Valentine's Day ballads, the St. Patrick's Day jigs. But, in a certain dormitory at St. Offal's, hanging in a small drainage pipe, there remains the link to the air raid sirens. Or so our source says.

GREAT BALLS OF FIRE

For those bullied by the jocks in their schools, a favorite and appropriate remedy has been found. Sneak into the locker room or have an accomplice on the inside thoroughly rub Ben-Gay, Absorbine Jr. or any other such ointment into the jockstrap of your tormentor. His time in the forty-yard dash should markedly improve.

IT SURE DOESN'T TASTE LIKE TOMATO JUICE

This legendary stunt is a long-standing favorite among practical jokers stuck in a hospital bed, forced to use a bedpan or specimen bottle. Take the specimen bottle or bedpan (which should be sterilized, but it's best to have an accomplice do this for you to be entirely safe). Fill the container with apple juice. When the doctor or nurse comes around to collect it, take the container, hold it up and say, "It looks the right color." Then drink half of it and say, "Yep, tastes the way it should." Hand the bottle to the nurse or doctor.

This prank can also be committed at your annual checkup, if a specimen has been requested. Taking a swig from the jar is just the thing to get the others in the waiting room distracted from their year-old copies of *National Geographic.*

TELEPHONE CLASSICS THE OLDEST OF THEM ALL

Out of the mothballs for perhaps its last appearance is this one:

Caller: Is your refrigerator running?
Target: Yes.
Caller: Well, you'd better go catch it!

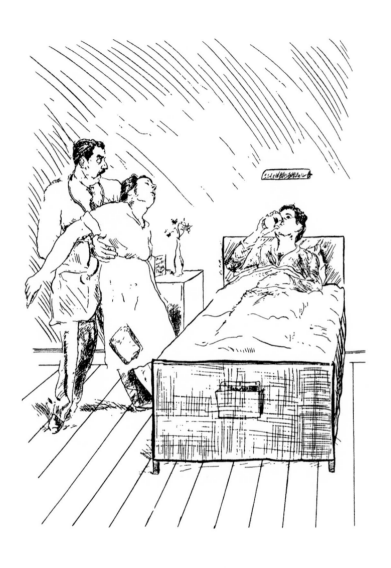

"It looks the right color."

ONCE MORE WITH FEELING

Any person who has attended a college with peers who plan on a career in medicine can attest that: (1) These students must all take a course in organic chemistry; (2) Many of these students are neurotic, compulsive, overachieving whiners; (3) These premed students make one wary of ever entering a hospital; (4) Their preoccupation with grades takes the fun out of a human being's life (just as later in life, the less capable of them will take the life out of human beings).

Circulate the following letter on college stationery to freshman premeds to get their year off to a rousing start.

Dear Premedical Student:

Welcome to (fill in name) College. We are happy to have you with us and wish you all the best for the coming year. During your four years here we hope you will take advantage of the many fine facilities and professors to prepare you for the career in medicine in which you have expressed interest.

We must inform you, however, that to be accepted in the premed courses at (fill in name) College, you must take our Premed Placement Examination. The exam is based on the science Achievement Tests of the Educational Testing Service and is designed to measure basic scientific aptitudes and the appropriateness of medicine as a career for freshmen.

The exam will be given two days from today at five o'clock at the (fill in name) Library [should be very far away]. It is the only time this year the test will be given. Even if you only are considering premed studies, it is wise to take this test.

We look forward to seeing you at the exam. Good luck.

Sincerely,

Dean of Freshmen

A possible variation is to include in the letter the information that study materials are available at a certain library on campus. When the frosh show up and find no materials you may enjoy the spectacle of seeing someone watch his nonexistent medical career go down the tubes.

AND NOW FOR A BRIEF INTERMISSION . . .

The following prank was committed in the middle of an extremely entertaining moment of reading and laughing. Rick and Tanya had purchased an outrageously funny book and were howling over each gag and humorous drawing. Then Rick paused and turned to Tanya. Clasping her bare shoulders with his firm, strong hands, he pulled her creamy willing flesh toward him. "Oh, Rick," Tanya sighed, rubbing his solid shoulders with her hot waxy hands, "you always know when to start." Tanya pushed his heaving chest back until she was astride him, gliding the moist, supple contours of her sweet, hungry body across his trembling torso. Rick licked the nape of her neck and—oh no! Sorry! Sorry! This isn't what we meant at all and it certainly isn't the reason you bought this excellent little book. You wanted jokes, not soft-core slime. We're terribly sorry, or at least a little sorry, but we thought you might enjoy a little jolt in the middle of this volume. Let's return to our book, already in progress, and we promise not to take advantage of your goodwill again.

FUNDAMENTAL VIOLATION OF PRIVACY

A decidedly lowbrow prank, this one is not for anyone with a responsible position in a fraternity, let alone a company. In any case, if you're in a silly mood, take a pair of speakers (the smaller, the better) and place them discreetly in the company washroom—in a ceiling corner, for example. Wire the speakers to a microphone in an equally discreet place. When a suitable target enters the bathroom for more than a brief visit, give the person enough time to get comfortable. Then, commence a series of rude noises and strange comments into the microphone—with the volume loud enough for persons outside the washroom to wonder what the hell George is doing in there and for George to wonder where the hell that noise is coming from.

A TIGHT SQUEEZE

Owners of Volkswagens and other small cars have often found themselves able to squeeze into parking spaces owners of larger cars cannot. This ability is tested, however, when the small car is parked in a lot with a car on each side. And several friends with some strength actually lift the car and turn it sideways so that the front and back of the car face the doors of the cars on each side.

This prank is extremely effective for dissuading someone from driving after he or she has had several cocktails, provided for course that this is not the sort of person who will gladly plow into the adjoining cars to get out of the space.

FRIEND OR ENEMA

One correspondent of ours thought the following a bit of knee-slapping fun. Having seen one obsequious, brown-nosing fellow student named Mark cheat on several tests, lie about his extracurricular activities and engage in other dishonorable acts to gain acceptance at an Ivy League college prompted our friend to telephone Mark three weeks before his departure for freshman year.

The conversation proceeded as follows:

"Hello, Mark. This is Dr. Roy Conway of University of Pennsylvania Health Services."

"Oh, hello, Dr. Conway. What can I do for you, sir?"

"Well, Mark, it seems as though you have a little problem. We recently passed a health ordinance here at the university, stipulating that all incoming fresh-

To dissuade someone from driving after a few cocktails.

men must have had a doctor-administered enema in the past three years before they can be admitted to their dorms. Well, I'm going over your health records, and I can't find any evidence that you have had an enema recently, fella."

"Gosh, what should I do, sir?"

"Well, Mark, if you want to be admitted to your dorm, you'll have to take care of this situation right away. Go to your family doctor and request the enema."

"Yes, sir. I certainly will. Sorry to inconvenience you, Dr. Conway."

"Not at all, Mark. Just take care of it, and we look forward to seeing you at U. Penn. in a couple of weeks, big guy."

It worked, we are told, and our correspondent adds that it seemed fair to give someone something that he'd given you for four years.

GO FORTH AND MULTIPLY

When the mother of four children of an Irish-Catholic American family announced her fifth pregnancy, her husband was sufficiently pleased and impressed with their mutual efforts to obtain through a friend some Vatican stationery. At a dinner party where they announced the coming of the fifth child, the husband passed his wife a letter to read out loud. It read:

Dear Mr. and Mrs. O'Connell:

On behalf of His Holiness the Pope and the Cardinals and the Saints, I would like to congratulate you on your pregnancy. Due to the increasing number of lapsed Catholics, we at the Vatican are currently paying close attention to those faithful members of the Church who replenish our numbers. Needless to say, you have certainly done your part to ensure the continuity of our religion as we know it. Bless you for your labors and know that your reward waits for you in Heaven.

Sincerely,

Cardinal Antonio Bambino

WIPING OUT THE OPPOSITION

Get even with rival fraternities, sororities or dormitories by making a stealthy raid on their bathrooms in the middle of the night. Remove all the toilet paper. By the middle of the morning, you should begin to see faces flushed with rage scurrying out of the target building.

IT HAPPENED THIS WAY, FELLAS

Our acquaintance Joan painted her husband's finger-nails while he was asleep and hid the nail polish remover. Her husband had to leave for work at 5 A.M. She left it to him to do the explaining to his colleagues.

THEY ALSO SQUIRM WHO ONLY STAND AND WAIT

An acquaintance from Ohio University recalls a room-mate—Jack—whose favorite pastime was to take a sports magazine into the only stall in the bathroom and relax for an hour or so after dinner each night. When friendly persuasion failed to change Jack's habits, his roommates took action.

They rigged a pair of jeans and sneakers inside the stall to appear as if someone were using the facilities, then locked the stall and crawled out under the door.

When Jack answered nature's call that night after dinner, he was disappointed to find that someone had beaten him to his well-established throne. Being a patient soul, Jack waited half an hour, going back and forth from his room to the bathroom, still to find the

But do his nails match his makeup?

stall occupied. Finally, after well more than an hour (we are informed that Jack was extremely devoted to his regular seat of honor), a flabbergasted Jack asked if the intruder was all right. When no response came, Jack became concerned and called campus security. When the security people arrived, they broke down the stall door, only to find the hanging jeans.

There is a marvelous postscript to this story. A few weeks later Jack was waiting to use the facility in one of his classroom buildings. After a seemingly endless wait, he decided his friends must be playing the same prank on him. So, not to be fooled, he crawled under the stall to remove the bogus clothing and use the toilet. As he lifted his head under the stall, he discovered that it was in fact occupied by a real person. His professor.

GHOSTBOOSTERS

To settle an old score with a classmate, two Princeton pranksters gained access to their target's room and attached speaker wire to his stereo speakers. Then, carefully concealing the wires under carpet and behind various objects, they ran the speaker wires out a window and back to their room.

When their target turned out his light at night to go to sleep, they played eerie music and sound effects into his stereo. As soon as the fellow awoke and turned on the light to investigate, the music and sound effects stopped. When the target returned to bed and turned the light out, the music and sound effects began again. Our source tells us that after the prank had gone on for some time, their friend finally ripped his speakers out of his stereo system.

An amusing variation for annoying premed or pre-law types is to substitute the eerie sound effects with recordings of their professors' lectures—particularly organic chemistry lectures for premeds. Then again, they may just lie in bed and take more notes.

USED CAR, ALMOST

If you have tired of listening to someone read you his back issues of *Car and Driver,* listing the virtues of the car he intends to buy, expounding upon the tremendous deal he cut with a car dealer across town ("and not a penny for air conditioning, quadraphonic stereo," etc.), how and where he intends to drive it, do not frown and ask him to kindly bugger off and stop asking when you are going to replace your clunker. Simply take out an ad in a local paper advertising your friend's car for sale the day it arrives at his house. Do not be unkind and say, "Call only after midnight."

A PENNY FOR YOUR THOUGHTLESSNESS

This prank is so well-established it is surprising that there is no exhibit of it at the Smithsonian in Washington, D.C. (The Smithsonian is a museum. A place where you go look at things, often very old.) Anyway, here it is:

With an accomplice and a target, demonstrate the following trick. You place a funnel in the waistband of your pants. Then, tilting your head back, you put a penny on your forehead. Next you tip your head forward, dropping the penny into the mouth of the funnel. (Some practice is involved; no one said it was going to be easy.)

Your accomplice demonstrates the trick as well. Finally comes your target's turn. He places the funnel in his pants, tips his head back and places the penny on his forehead, and—*voilà!*—ice water from a nearby pitcher is poured down the funnel into his pants.

A favorite variation among practitioners is to enlist the aid of an enthusiastic accomplice, who, as he demonstrates the trick, receives the ice water instead of the target.

101

DIAMONDS ARE FOREVER

If you know of a man who is being uncommonly mean to a girlfriend who has been uncommonly good to him, or vice versa, send the woman a fake diamond ring and a short note proposing marriage from the boyfriend. It's a handy technique for prompting a little honesty out of a relationship.

WHERE'S THE KITCHEN SINK?

Practical jokers who work at places that have a security guard at a main gate have enjoyed numerous occasions of mirth with this stunt. During the day, ask to borrow a colleague's car keys to perform some routine errand. Then load up the victim's trunk with several office typewriters, a chair, office supplies, several telephones, company tools and any other property belonging to the firm. Return the individual's keys. At quitting time, telephone the main gate and inform the security guard that you've seen some suspicious behavior by someone driving your friend's car and that it might be a good idea for the guard to check the fellow's trunk. After playing this joke, it is probably unwise to lend your car or ask to borrow another's.

"Bringing work home from the office, fella?"

THE BELLS ARE RINGING

A small prank enjoyed by many is taping down one of the buttons in the cradle of the telephone, so that when someone picks up the ringing phone, the telephone continues to ring. This stunt works especially well if the phone has several extensions. As the phone rings, the target continues to press the button for a different line to no avail.

PARTY TO THE CRIME

To show his sister's ex-boyfriend, Tad, that there were no hard feelings after Tad cruelly dumped the sweet girl, Stuart invited the fellow to a party at his apartment. "Come around seven-thirty. Very casual," he told Tad.

When Tad arrived in jeans at seven-thirty, Stuart acted surprised but welcomed him. After a half hour of chatting he excused himself to fix things up, since, he said, "The guests will be arriving at nine-thirty." Naturally, Tad apologized for coming early, but added, "I thought you said seven-thirty."

"Gee, I didn't think so," said Stuart, "but don't worry." After an hour of showering, changing and letting his guest stew unattended, Stuart returned dressed in a tuxedo.

"Is everyone going to be as dressed up as you?" asked Tad. "I thought this was a casual affair."

"Don't worry about it," said Stuart. "Could you help me set things up?"

At nine-thirty the guests began to arrive, all dressed in formal attire. As they came in, each handed Stuart a small, attractively wrapped present. "Happy Birthday, Stuart," each guest said. Two hours early, dressed in the wrong clothes, with no present for his host, Tad shriveled in his chair, shrinking with embarrassment each time Stuart introduced a guest to him.

In addition to being used as a tool for social mortification, this prank has been used to begin a surprise party for the target. In this case, the guests are instructed to bring gifts for the target, but pretend that they are for the host. At the point when the target's embarrassment meter is well in the red, the host and guests bring out the cake. Upon realizing the setup, many targets take the cake and plow it into the host's face.

TIME TO KILL

One golf widow grew tired of her weekly abandonment and her husband's 8 A.M. tee-off times. The Friday night before a major club tournament, he set the alarm for six o'clock and advised his wife, "Make sure I get up in time."

After he fell asleep, she set *both* the clock and the alarm two hours ahead. When her husband awoke, apparently two hours behind schedule, Alice smiled while George cursed and raced around. As a small act of charity, she advised him to look at his wrist watch as he headed half-dressed out the door. She made her point.

A FEW DIRTY LINES

As one of the members of the rock group Spinal Tap says, "There's often a very fine line between cleverness and stupidity." And so it goes with this telephone prank—either cleverly weird or plain dumb, depending on the circumstances. We do know that it has worked well on many occasions.

Telephone someone in your office and say you are from the phone company and are currently cleaning out the telephone lines. "So would you please leave your phone off the hook and step away from your desk for the next five minutes to avoid any mess?" you ask. Once they agree, observe the person stepping away from his desk. Have an accomplice distract them if necessary. Then leave small circles of dust and dirt by the mouth- and earpiece of the person's telephone receiver. When they return and see the results, they will experience a baffling sense of unease.

BLIND DATE

Expanding upon a practical joke committed by a group of University of Virginia women, we offer appropriate justice for those rude persons who fail to return phone calls, stand up their dates and are generally thoughtless. Our friend Mary assures us that this stunt can work.

She and her friends begin by calling one of the men who has treated one of them rudely. A voice the man is unfamiliar with makes the call and says something like, "Hi, this is Tracey. Tracey *Adams*. Oh my God, you mean you don't remember. I met you last weekend at Sigma Chi, and we had such a good time, and you told me to call you, and now I'm so embarrassed." Of course, while the fellow *was* at Sigma Chi last weekend, Tracey Adams is an invented name. Nonetheless, according to Mary, all of their targets pretended to remember. Several offered to meet that night at a bar. What she does is agree to meet within an hour or so. She then calls other rotters, plays out her Tracey Adams routine. If they don't ask her out that night, she suggests a rendezvous at the same bar as she told the other fellow and makes the date for the same time.

When a sufficient number of targets (and their fraternity brothers) have been called and set up, she and her friends wait in a corner of the bar. When the targets have assembled and have stewed in their juices for a while, one of the girls goes to a nearby pay phone and calls the bar. She instructs the bartender to ask, "Is someone waiting for a call from Tracey Adams?" Her friends watch a crowd make their way to the phone and say to each other, "I believe that call is for me." "Uh, no, I believe that call is for *me.*" And finally, "Wait a minute, fellas."

SPECIAL DELIVERY

Several acquaintances of ours who, fortunately, live many miles away decided to celebrate a friend's birthday by delivering a very large present to him: his own car. Having filched his keys from his jacket, Tom and Roy drove his car from the parking lot to a waiting forklift belonging to their company. They hoisted the car onto a truck they had commandeered and promptly delivered the car to the company's loading dock, where they deposited it. They then returned to their office and dropped their friend's keys into his coat pocket.

Later that morning Joel received a call from the company warehouse saying that a large package had been delivered to him and would he mind picking it up since it was blocking the loading dock. Understandably curious, Joel went over to the warehouse only to find his car waiting for him with a birthday note. The next question, however, was how to get the car down off the loading dock.

SERIOUSLY THOUGH, MR. KHRUSHCHEV

At Harvard College there exists a long-standing rivalry between the Harvard *Crimson*, the daily student newspaper, and the Harvard *Lampoon*, a humor magazine. The *Crimson* alleges that, among other things, members of the *Lampoon* have stolen entire editions of the *Crimson* by arriving at drop-off depots before the delivery boys and girls. The *Lampoon* alleges that, among other things, the *Crimson* has in the past stolen their mascot, an ibis—or stork, to regular folks— which graced the entrance to their building. For many years, the ibis was not welded to the building and was stolen from time to time, appearing in the corners of photographs in the *Crimson*—a silent way of saying, "Na-na-nana-na, we've got your ibis."

The stealing of the ibis reached its peak when a member of the *Crimson* presented the stolen bird to a visiting Soviet dignitary as a "gift of friendship and goodwill from American students to Soviet students." The Soviet diplomat left with a bird in hand. Embarrassed, the *Lampoon* had to recall its mascot from overseas. East-West relations continued apace. The bird was welded to the *Lampoon*'s building.

FISHING LINE II

A small amount of mischief can be had in your office or at a party by attaching fishing line to a target's chair and tieing it to an object on his desk or at the table. Thus, when the target pulls out his chair, the attached object is set in motion, bumping into whatever stands in its path. Attaching the line to a water jug, ashtray or files can create momentary mayhem as your target takes his seat. Naturally, a heightened effect can be gained by attaching the line to several chairs and a variety of objects at a dinner table. As guests sit down, you will create a spectacle that would even astonish Uri Geller.

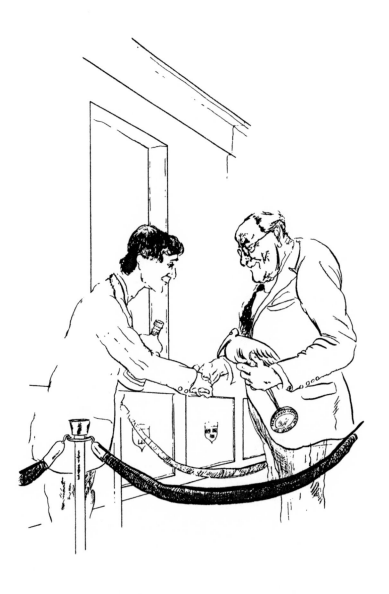

"The pleasure is ours, Mr. Khrushchev."

HARK! THE HERALD ANGEL SPEAKS

This practical joke is purely whacky college hijinx, but the technical expertise involved does command some respect. Railing against the excessive seriousness of the premedical students in their organic chemistry class, two Princeton sophomores, William and Tim, spent several evenings rewiring the intercom system of the lecture hall where the course was given.

On the given day, the two students assumed their seats in the lecture hall from where they operated a tape deck connected to the auditorium's speakers. Just as the professor was about to begin the lecture, the hall was filled with the "Star Trek" theme and the ominous pronouncement, "Organic chemistry . . . the final frontier." Having anticipated that their professor would discuss the "Gabriel synthesis," (a theoretical aspect of organic chemistry we are very interested in not discussing), Will and Tim played the taped voice of the angel Gabriel rebuking the scholar for revealing this divine secret. A host of other sound effects, a specially composed song and a mechanically unveiled portrait of the professor were part of the festivities. So, ho-ho-ho. Clever sophomores, you say, but still sophomoric?

112

Consider the following. Tapes of God arguing creationism in a biology class. Winston Churchill, John F. Kennedy and other historical figures defending themselves or speaking up during lectures on them. (See "Name That Tune" for another variation for political events.)

WHO CUT THE CHEESE?

Limburger cheese, well-known for its pungent aroma, is an effective room-clearing ingredient when applied to a hot radiator or steam pipe. Since the smell of Limburger lingers for a good while, it is advisable not to pull this stunt in an area that you will be frequenting on a very regular basis. Other long-standing favorite variations are hiding a carton of cream by a radiator and letting nature take its course. The resulting smell will make your target's blood curdle. And finally, sea or swamp water filled with algae, seaweed and other decomposing matter can be applied to facial tissue and left in a target's wastebasket while he or she is at lunch. Your colleague will think something's more than fishy upon arrival.

THROW THE BOOK AT 'EM

A man married to an incurable practical joker has passed on this prank for evening the score and maintaining his version of marital harmony.

Walk into a store—a bookstore, for example—in a shopping mall. Politely ask to see the manager. "Pardon me," you say to the manager, "but I manage a store at the other end of the mall, and lately we've had problems with a woman in a blue-and-red dress who's been shoplifting. And not only from us, but from other stores in the mall, too. I don't mean to tell you your business, but I just wanted to advise you of the problem."

"Thanks for the warning," the happily informed manager will reply.

You continue. "It's funny—from looking at her you would never think she's the type that would do this sort of thing, but who understands these things anyway?" You give a further description of the shoplifter, then leave.

One hour later you say to your target, who is wearing a blue-and-red dress and fits the description you gave the store manager, "I'll meet you in the bookstore in the mall at three o'clock."

(Naturally, this prank works for either sex, as long as

*"We've had problems with a woman in a
blue-and-red dress who's been shoplifting."*

you can describe the target sharply enough so that he or she is easily identified when entering the bookstore.)

Now, you can leave it at that and simply watch your target enter the bookstore and see the reaction of the store manager, or do the following. Say to your target, "And, by the way, if you get to the store before me, could you please pick up these books?" You read a list of books and say, "Don't bother paying for them. It's a business expense, and I'll need my credit card."

From an unseen vantage point, watch the fun in the store begin.

When the prank is over, buy a copy of this book for your friend to show there are no hard feelings.

MORE SHAVING CREAM

You are the victim of a cheap, unprovoked practical joke. Moments ago you were a law-abiding citizen with a respect for other persons and the law. But now you want swift revenge. But your tormentor is hiding behind a sturdy locked door. There is little you can do at the moment unless there is a small gap between the bottom of his door and the floor. Well, no problem. Simply take a large manila envelope and fill it with shaving cream. Place the open end of the envelope under the door. Jump on the envelope near its end, and you will propel a steady stream of foam across your enemy's room. If this irritating person is laughing him- or herself to sleep, you may wish to substitute whipped cream or topping, which, unlike shaving cream, will start to turn rancid by morning.

RETURN OF THE BLOB

For the person in your life who has caused you endless delays, late arrivals and hours sitting in your underwear getting cold because this person cannot take a bath under two hours in duration, the following remedy has been suggested to us. Buy ten packs of clear gelatin. Fill the tub with the appropriate amount of water. Throw in enough ice to set the mixture. Replace the bathroom light with a low-wattage bulb. Wait for the person to step into the tub. For diversity, flavored gelatin can be used, particularly in shower stalls.

If, say, you have recently lost a job because of a housemate's interminable baths, you may enhance the prank by lighting a candle in the bathroom and steaming up the mirror with hot water from the sink. When your friend/lover/enemy returns home, tell him you've prepared the perfect remedy for a hard day and lead him into the waiting goo.

DO I EXIST?

One of the lesser-known but classic practical jokes is the room-vanishing act. While at college, Fred decided to spend the weekend visiting his girlfriend at a school in the next state. That Saturday his neighbors in the dorm obtained a key to his room and removed the door from its hinges. Plasterboard was put in its place, the edges were sealed with putty and the entire wall in the hallway was given a fresh coat of paint. Any trace of a room having been there had vanished. When Fred returned he spent hours walking up and down the hall wondering what had happened to his room. The effect of this elaborate but remarkable prank is disorienting, especially if played on philosophy students who, after going from floor to floor trying to figure out where exactly they are, will ask themselves, "Do I really exist?"

SOCKET TO THEM

A frisky seminarian friend of ours extended his future stay in purgatory by several years by playing this prank on a roommate. Returning late one night to his apartment, the fellow turned on the light switch, only to find himself still in the dark. Instead of light, the whine of an electric floor polisher erupted as the machine went berserk, swirling across the living room floor, banging into furniture.

According to our seminarian, a pet duck happened to be asleep on top of the floor polisher, which was plugged into the empty light socket. When the target flipped the switch and the polisher sprang to life, the noise so startled the poor creature that it literally frightened the "duck soup" out of it, "soup" that was promptly polished into the bare wooden floor.

Between the quacking of the duck and the racket of the floor polisher, the surprised roommate wondered whether he was in fact witnessing the tribulations of the Second Coming.

There are a number of variations on this theme of plugging appliances into light sockets from which the bulb has been removed.

(1) To repay the perpetrator of the above prank or for other seminarians, plug the tape deck into the light socket or appropriate outlet. Have the tape deck set at "Play," loaded with a cassette. When the target enters the room and flips on the light switch, the tape will be activated, playing your prerecorded message, such as, "Fred, this is the Lord. Why do you turn on the light when you walk in the darkness? I have been watching you, Fred, and your sins have not escaped me." You can then include some recent transgression and any other directives you deem fitting.

119

(2) You may wish to prerecord other sounds or messages—a couple in the throes of passion, then your voice: "Fred, I have someone with me. Do you mind stepping out for a bit?" The sounds of farm animals are suitably bizarre; a recording of barking dogs is starting to push things, however.

"WILD KINGDOM" COMES TO COLLEGE

Several party animals at a college south of the Mason-Dixon Line thought it somewhat incongruous that their college's natural history museum was located above the campus security headquarters. As a combination prank/dare, a group of students scaled the fire escape of the museum in the middle of the night. When they reached the second floor, they climbed through a window they had unlocked that day during an afternoon visit to the museum. (Yes, hard to believe as it is, the museum did not have an alarm and did not thoroughly lock its windows at night.)

They proceeded to remove eight of the museum's stuffed animals, including a gorilla, seal and black bear. Then, descending the fire escape above the campus police, hauling their taxidermic specimens, they distributed the animals around campus. The gorilla assumed watch in the campus bell tower (without Fay

"As Jim and I made our way up the river and across campus . . ."

Wray); the bear took temporary hibernation in front of the college administration building; the seal was placed in front of the college president's house, with the card "Presidential Seal" next to it. The next day, calls to the campus police informed them of wild animals loose on the college grounds. Given the nature of the students at this school, it is fair to say that the abducted creatures had briefly returned to their natural habitat.

I DON'T HAVE A THING TO WEAR

For those persons who borrow your clothes without asking, who delay you endlessly because they can't decide which of twelve outfits they should wear to a garage sale, who laugh and sneer at your wardrobe, there is a simple remedy. Simply wait until they are in the shower or bath on an evening when they are not going out with you and remove all their clothes from their room and hide them. For some individuals with a wardrobe the size of a warehouse, you will have to enlist a host of accomplices to get the job done. Remove the towels, too. What you give back—and when —is up to you.

CAUGHT WITH HIS HAND IN THE COOKIE JAR

This practical joke is a favorite among schoolgirls who have to put up with the macho performances of certain male teachers. One high school coed stuck with a male chemistry teacher who assumed that every girl in the class was after him began by sending her target a carnation.

It was close to Easter, so she signed the accompanying card "With love and devotion, the Easter Bunny." Though he could not identify the sender, he placed the carnation in a jar on his desk in the front of the class.

Several days later, the Easter Bunny struck again, this time leaving a note and a plate of cookies on the target's desk at the front of the class.

The teacher read the note, smirked and began his lab class.

When he thought no one was looking, he walked over to the plate of cookies, picked one up and took a huge bite. Then he bit into another. Yet, just as he bit into the second of his oatmeal cookies, he came to the grim realization that they had been liberally dosed with cayenne pepper. With flames pouring out of his mouth, he raced out of the classroom, providing a

123

vivid demonstration of the chemistry principle that if you increase temperature, you increase the velocity of particles. Or something like that.

Our source for this prank notes that since cayenne pepper is dark and a good deal of it is needed to get the desired effect, it is best to make a half batch of cookies and to make a "dark" cookie, such as oatmeal, to hide the powder.

TRY TO TALK YOUR WAY OUT OF THIS ONE

Friends who boast that they can talk their way out of speeding tickets, talk their way into any private club and sell ice to the Eskimos are excellent candidates for this routine. Find an accomplice (we'll call her Janis) and inform her of your plan. Then approach the "big talker" and perform the following routine:

> You (to Big Talker): Did you know that Janis's father is a concert pianist? He's extremely talented.
>
> Big Talker: No, I didn't.
>
> You: He is. You should ask Janis about it. It's a fascinating story. You should hear it.
>
> Big Talker: Yeah, I will.
> (Several minutes elapse. Big Talker approaches Janis, the accomplice.)

Big Talker: Janis, I hear your father is an excellent
        pianist. (Janis gapes in horror at the Big Talker,
        then speaks in hushed, hurt, insulted tones.)
Janis (Your Accomplice):   How could you say that?
        My father has no hands.

A person's response to this news is highly revealing
of their character, especially if they snicker.

SEX WITHOUT FEELING
IS AN EMPTY EXPERIENCE

Our source for this prank is an outraged female whose
college roommate had betrayed her. Our friend Joan
had poured open her heart to her roommate Anne,
telling her how much she wanted to date Robert, a boy
in their class they both had met. Robert was friendly
and had gladly accepted an invitation to a party the
girls were throwing in their dorm. Anne listened to
Joan's appraisal of her chances of hitting it off with
Robert and wished her luck. The day of the party,
Anne helped Joan select her clothes and fix her hair.
The night of the party, while Joan was replacing re-
freshments, Anne took Robert out for a stroll. When
Joan returned home after the party, wondering what
had happened to her alleged friends, she found a note
asking her if she minded sleeping in the living room. It
wasn't until the morning when Anne and Robert

emerged from the bedroom that Joan learned of the betrayal.

Joan contained herself in the days that followed as the affair continued. She did, however, replace Anne's lubricating jelly with topical anesthetic, a laborious and time-consuming process but worth it in the long run. "Robert is the most inept lover in the world," said Anne two weeks later when she dumped him.

BUT IS IT ART? or
MAN RAY REVISITED

At a recent art exhibition at a museum, two friends of ours with somewhat classic tastes were appalled by a number of contemporary pieces—a pile of bricks on the floor, a stove with a pot on it and other forms of artistic expression on the banal fringe of modernism. In short, they didn't like the exhibit. Not one bit.

To express their displeasure, they returned to their art studio and prepared title cards—with the name of the artist and the title of the work—in the same format used by the museum. They then returned to the museum and stuck these cards next to various objects. Over a thermostat, they placed a card which read, "Frank Durbin 1948–, American, *Temperature Rising.*" Beside a fire extinguisher the card "Jules Caldwell, 1922–1980, American, *Extinguisher II.*"

*The card read, "Jules Caldwell, 1922–1980,
American, Extinguisher II."*

According to the pranksters, the cards stayed up several days before the museum noticed—and, no doubt, confirmed with a curator that these were not part of the exhibit.

PROMOTIONAL SERVICES PROVIDED BY . . .

Working in a highly competitive office environment can be extremely stressful. If this is the case in your current situation, provide a little levity the next time a position for a better job becomes available by circulating the memo below to a half dozen of your colleagues. Sign it using the name of the appropriate manager:

MEMO

As you are no doubt aware, the position of (fill in the appropriate job) is open. After reviewing all the possible candidates it's clear that you are the best possible choice for the job. Your recent work has been superior, despite whatever small qualifications or comments have been made. It's clear to me that as far as your growth in the company is concerned, this job is an appropriate and necessary step in your career, one which I am sure will continue to lead to bigger and better things. We have big plans in store for you if you're willing to take on the job.

It's important that we speak right away. There-fore, could you please see me in my office at three o'clock today. Please wait if I'm on the phone or have someone in my office. Also, I'm sure you understand how important it is not to mention or show this memo to anyone—even me—until we meet. We don't want to ruffle any feathers. Congratulations and keep up the fine work.

To reduce suspicion, send the memo to yourself. Show up at the appointment and ask the others what they're waiting for.

REACH OUT AND TORTURE SOMEONE II, or THE WICHITA LINEMAN IS DEAD ON THE LINE

This practical joke is not only amusing, it is also a test of an individual's moral fiber. Call an acquaintance and say, "Hello, I'm from the telephone company, and we are experiencing some serious short-circuiting in the lines that may disrupt the entire system in your area. Some repairmen are going to start working on the problem in a few minutes. We must ask you though not to pick up the phone if it should ring, because, if you do, you'll complete the circuit and electrocute the lineman."

After hanging up, call the person back. If they show a good conscience and resist picking up, call them again in a minute or two. Continued refusal to pick up the phone indicates that this person is a model citizen and fine human being. This result occurs one in a hundred times. The more common case is for the person to ignore your warning and pick up the phone when it rings. When they do so, shout into the receiver, "Aaaiiieeeeeee!" as if a few thousand volts were passing through your body. Beware of any persons who respond to your electrocution with the word "Suffer!"

YOUR HEAD ON A PLATTER, or JOHN THE BAPTIST & SALOME II

This macabre party joke requires a table with removable leaves, a tablecloth with a hole in it, three balls, four towels or large napkins and some makeup. An accomplice hides under the table and sticks his head through the opened space between the leaves of the table and through the hole in the tablecloth. His or her face should be made up in as horrifying a manner as possible—as if a victim of the guillotine.

The three balls are placed on the table near the accomplice's head and all four objects are covered with the towels or napkins. The first target is brought into the room and told he must guess what kinds of balls (e.g., volleyball, basketball, soccer ball) are hidden under the towels within a certain time limit. When they are finished guessing, the three towels covering the actual balls are removed before finally exposing the "decapitated head."

The prank should be repeated with a second target, and then finally a third. This third target, however, is given a cream pie, so that upon completion of the stunt, the accomplice beneath the table receives a pie in the face—his just desserts, so to speak.

I CAN EXPLAIN EVERYTHING, DEAR

A number of states have laws against sexual harassment. Certain companies have explicit internal policies that deal with this annoying and demeaning problem. But filing a complaint is often expensive and more harmful in the long run to the victim instead of the offender. One group of Pennsylvania women dealt with their office grabber in a much swifter and amusing manner.

Ron, one of the salesmen in their printing office, was constantly approaching the women with a variety of unsavory offers and proposals, all suggested with an

"Just having lunch with a few friends, dear."

assortment of pats and squeezes. With his lecherous smile, he would invite them to topless bars where, it was said, he was on more than a speaking relationship with a number of the local dancers. As with most mashers, he would insist that his come-ons were all in good fun—unless, of course, he was alone with one of the women.

When Ron's birthday rolled around, one of the women who had rebuffed him suggested that she and another woman in the office take him out for lunch. He agreed and they drove to one of his favorite sleazy bars, where they met another woman from the office in the parking lot. She got in the car, and they started driving away.

"Where are we going?" asked Ron.

"Just wait and see, big boy," purred one of the girls in the back seat, draping a hand over his knee.

Ten minutes later, they pulled into the parking lot of the El Coyote Motel, a local establishment specializing in nooners and rooms for rent by the hour. The women were aware that Ron was a somewhat regular customer. What they didn't know was that the room they had rented was the one he habitually reserved.

Now, at this point, Ron is clearly of two minds. Part of him thinks he's hit the jackpot; the other realizes what kind of guy he is and says, "This has to be a joke." When the car comes to a stop, Ron asks, "Seriously, where are we going?"

"Right here," says one of the women, showing him

the room key and winking. Ron stares at the room number, amazed. There must be a God, he thinks.

With a basket full of food, the four go into the motel room. The women drape themselves across the bed with a sultry swish. "How about some food before we get down to dessert," croons one of the girls. Ron salivates.

Meanwhile, working with the women, two male colleagues at the office call Ron's wife and inform her of the setup, and ask her to join them at the motel shortly after her husband arrives. It is not known to what degree she was aware of her husband's escapades.

She agrees and arrives at the motel. Then, standing at the motel room door, she knocks and calls in a stern, perplexed voice, "Ron? Ron? Are you in there? Come out right now! Don't pretend you don't know who this is. Come out now!"

Inside, Ron spits up a mouthful of food, grabs his coat and heads to the door, which he flings open. He faces his wife and a photographer who captures his gaping, stunned expression for posterity.

"I can explain everything, dear," he whines. "This isn't what it looks like."

"Neither is this," says his wife, as all the accomplices reveal themselves.

Naturally, one can get nastier and omit to tell the wife that you are playing a practical joke, and simply get her over there, but remember that the idea is not to hurt the innocent.

GEE, DAD . . . DAD?!

In childlike script, send Father's Day cards to womanizing louts that say, "You do not know me, but my name is Jason, and I would like to meet you, since you are my father. Mommy is helping me write this letter, since I am only three years old. I will call you soon or come by your office next week. Your son, Jason."

HITTING THE CEILING

Though substantial preparation is involved for this classic, its effect on your target, particularly a stranger, is considerable. Conceptually, this practical joke is simple: Attach all of your target's furniture to the ceiling. In practice, this is a good deal more complicated, since a little engineering savvy is required to do the job correctly. Nonetheless, for those pranksters so inclined, the effort is more than worth it.

A variation on this stunt—and one we actually prefer—is to attach *one's own* office furniture to the ceiling and to invite various individuals in for interviews. Upon entering your office, the target discovers you seated upside down at your desk. (You will have belted yourself to the chair and glued your blotter, pen set and papers to the table.) Then commence an interview with your visitor. Invite the person to be seated at the empty chair attached to the ceiling. Pull open a file drawer next to your desk. With papers glued to the files and the files glued to the drawer, the papers will seemingly defy gravity as you remove them. You'll have to make the interview short, of course, since hanging upside down for long periods of time is not too pleasant.

Our research informs us that the main practitioners of this stunt are owners of small businesses. Regrettably, New York investment banks and corporations such as IBM take a dim view of on-the-job frivolity such as this.

A FISH STORY

For gentle wit and symmetry, this practical joke is hard to beat. A young woman named Cindy worked as a secretary in an art department. One day she brought a goldfish to work and placed it in a bowl on her desk. In the days that followed, she fed the fish regularly. After a week, she noticed that the fish had grown half an inch. In a few days, her goldfish had grown another half inch. The fish continued to grow every few days. What Cindy didn't know was that the art directors, Tom and Roy, were changing the fish every few days, putting larger and larger fish in the bowl.

After several weeks, when it seemed that the gold-fish might outgrow the bowl, Tom and Roy suggested that Cindy feed the fish less. She agreed, and after a few days the fish began to shrink back to its initial size. For nearly a month, Cindy watched her fish expand and contract, never for a minute wondering how fish bones shrink. All right, so this won't work on everybody. But it *is* a true story.

BUT WAS IT A GOOD READ?

A very effective prank that many authors could use at publishing parties is to affix covers of their books with a strong glue or extremely sticky tape. Thus, when they pass out copies of their books to reviewers and colleagues, the recipients of the books will literally have a book that they cannot put down. Though such a stunt will increase the chances of the critics seeing one's book, the question of favorable reviews does arise.

FLOOR PLAN

A Boston University student, Karen, and her friend Rod created this amusing effect the night of a campus dance. Purchasing materials to make exact replicas of

I just couldn't put the book down!

the number plates on their dorm rooms, they returned to their high-rise dormitory, made the plates and waited for the dance to begin. Then they changed each one on the tenth floor to room numbers of the thirteenth—1301, 1302, etc.

On each of the doors leading to the stairwells they placed signs that read, "Warning: Alarm. Emergency Use Only." The bulletin boards on the floor were removed and replaced with new ones containing fictitious notes and notices, birthday wishes and announcements of upcoming "floor meetings."

As the primary target of the prank was Karen's roommate Diane, Karen had surreptitiously switched her roommate's room key with an accomplice's just before Diane left for the dance. Thus, if Diane tried to get back into her room without paying attention to the new room number, the key would not work.

Karen and Rod had accomplices at the dance alert them when Diane and her date left to return to her room. Then the two pranksters locked themselves in the room and waited for their target's arrival.

At first, it seemed to Diane and her date that the elevators had stopped on the wrong floor—thirteen instead of ten. But when she got back in and pressed "ten" again, the doors opened. Thinking themselves clever, they pushed "thirteen" and promptly rode up three floors and discovered a second thirteenth floor. After several trips back and forth, they rode to the ninth floor and walked up the stairwell. Ignoring the sign not to open the door to the thirteenth floor, Diane and her date found themselves once more on a strange floor with unfamiliar bulletin boards and room numbers.

Persisting all the same, she tried to unlock the room she thought was hers—despite the number change—and found that the lock did not work. For a moment, she wondered whether she was in the wrong building. Finally she saw a familiar face (the rest of the students on the floor were in on the gag) sneaking out of a room. Following her into the bathroom, Diane saw familiar articles and the prank was over.

The confusion and amusement created by this practical joke can be heightened, but it means more work. After replacing the tenth-floor room numbers with those of the thirteenth, one could replace the numbers of the eleventh, twelfth and thirteenth floors with those numbers for floors fourteen, fifteen and sixteen, respectively. So, if your target finds that his tenth floor is really the thirteenth and decides to go up one floor to check things out, he will soon find himself on the fourteenth floor. Don't forget to post the signs by the stairwells above and below the floor. That way, should your target find himself on the ninth floor and decide to walk up, he will risk the embarrassment of pulling the alarm. Instead, he will get on the elevator, push "ten," and find himself on floor thirteen—three floors of campus residence having evaporated.

Or you might care to make the tenth floor the eleventh floor and the ninth floor the tenth. Then switch your target's keys for the appropriate room on the ninth. (You'll have to find an accomplice for this.) After an evening of cocktails, your target may be somewhat surprised to return to a radically different room than the one he left.

GUILT BY ASSOCIATION

A small but delightful prank is to address letters to friends, relatives or enemies with improbable names of organizations or actual organizations whose goals are diametrically opposed to the recipient. "Friends of the Ayatollah c/o John Doe," "Businessmen for Social Revolution," "Actresses for Nuclear Weapons" and "Communists for Christ" are just a few examples of what is possible. Naturally, the prank is enhanced when it is delivered to an office or home where a number of persons will see it. Before mailing such letters you may wish to consider your target's sense of humor since libel laws do extend to matters such as this. Instead, you may decide to put someone you know on the mailing lists of political parties, special interest groups and assorted lunatics whom he abhors.

MOST EFFECTIVE OF ALL

When all else fails, there's always this stunt. Be nice to people. Treat them courteously and with respect. If you are snubbed or treated rudely, do not take this personally. Regard it as a reflection on the other person and not yourself. Express your displeasure or annoyance in straightforward, even tones, then get on with your business, being helpful and considerate when you can. Don't take yourself seriously, but be serious about what you do. Write thank-you notes and always be on time. Forgive your enemies. This behavior is shocking to most people, since many are unfamiliar with it. By pursuing such a course, thousands will grovel in fear, wondering when you're really going to act like yourself. By following these basic guidelines, you are likely to get much of what you want. Yeah, sure. No, seriously, we mean it. At least, we'd like to mean it.

WE'D LIKE TO HEAR FROM YOU!

YOU MIGHT HAVE YOUR NAME PUBLISHED IN OUR NEXT VOLUME OF PRACTICAL JOKES!

Thanks for reading this book. You loved it? We're glad to hear it. But what? It wasn't quite as complete as it might have been? You know some good practical jokes not contained on these pages? Better than these? Well, let's not get personal about it. Let's just say that we'd like to hear from you with your best pranks, stunts, outrageous and atrocious acts. Write to us at the address below with a typed or neatly written account of all your exploits. And no funny business, please. We're experts at this. Besides, this book is about evening the score, not starting a vendetta. Include the coupon below with your submission. Don't worry, we won't pull anything on you either, nor will your name be distributed to any advertiser or group of shady characters. We promise. So, don't just sit there—write us today!

—Justin Geste

NATIONAL PRACTICAL JOKES II

Name _____

Address _____

City _____ State _____ Zip _____

Phone _(___)_____

Mail all entries to: National Practical Jokes

P.O. Box 6560

F.D.R. Station

New York, NY 10150

Printed in the United States
65783LVS00003B/95